NARCISSISM

OTHER BOOKS BY ALEXANDER LOWEN:

Fear of Life

The Way to Vibrant Health

Bioenergetics

Depression and the Body

Pleasure: A Creative Approach to Life

Betrayal of the Body

Love and Orgasm

The Language of the Body

NARCISSISM

DENIAL OF THE TRUE SELF

Alexander Lowen, M.D.

COLLIER BOOKS
Macmillan Publishing Company
New York

COLLIER MACMILLAN PUBLISHERS
London

Macmillan Publishing Company.
866 Third Avenue, New York, N.Y. 10022
Collier Macmillan Canada, Inc.

Library of Congress Cataloging in Publication Data
Lowen, Alexander.
Narcissism : denial of the true self.
Includes bibliographical references and index.
1. Narcissism. 2. Bioenergetic psychotherapy.
I. Title.
[RC553.N36L68 1985] 616.85'82 84-9579
ISBN 0-02-077290-4 (pbk.)

First Collier Books Edition 1985

10 9 8 7 6 5 4

Designed by Jack Meserole

Narcissim: Denial of the True Self is also published in a hardcover edition by Macmillan Publishing Company.

Printed in the United States of America

CONTENTS

ACKNOWLEDGMENTS

I WISH to express my thanks to Dr. Michael Conant and Mirra Ginsburg, who read parts of the manuscript and offered some helpful suggestions; to Marion Wheeler, editor at Macmillan, whose advice greatly strengthened this study; and to Ruth MacKenzie of the International Institute for Bioenergetic Analysis, who graciously typed and retyped the manuscript.

INTRODUCTION

NARCISSISM describes both a psychological and a cultural condition. On the individual level, it denotes a personality disturbance characterized by an exaggerated investment in one's image at the expense of the self. Narcissists are more concerned with how they appear than what they feel. Indeed, they deny feelings that contradict the image they seek. Acting without feeling, they tend to be seductive and manipulative, striving for power and control. They are egotists, focused on their own interests but lacking the true values of the self—namely, self-expression, self-possession, dignity, and integrity. Narcissists lack a sense of self derived from body feelings. Without a solid sense of self, they experience life as empty and meaningless. It is a desolate state.

On the cultural level, narcissism can be seen in a loss of human values—in a lack of concern for the environment, for the quality of life, for one's fellow human beings. A society that sacrifices the natural environment for profit and power betrays its insensitivity to human needs. The proliferation of material things becomes the measure of progress in living, and man is pitted against woman, worker against employer, individual against community. When wealth occupies a higher position than wisdom, when notoriety is admired more than dignity, when success is more important than self-respect, the culture itself overvalues "image" and must be regarded as narcissistic.

The narcissism of the individual parallels that of the culture. We shape our culture according to our image and in turn we are shaped by that culture. Can we understand one without understanding the other? Can psychology ignore sociology, or vice versa?

In the forty years I have worked as a therapist, I have seen a marked change in the personality problems of the people consulting me. The neuroses of earlier times, represented by incapacitating guilts, anxieties, phobias, or obsessions, are not commonly seen today. Instead, I see more people who complain of depression; they describe a lack of feeling, an inner emptiness, a deep sense of frustration and unfulfillment. Many are quite successful in their work, which suggests a split between the way they perform in the world and what goes on inside. What seems rather strange is a relative absence of anxiety and guilt, despite the severity of the disturbance. This absence of anxiety and guilt, coupled with an absence of feeling, gives one an impression of unreality about these people. Their performance—socially, sexually, and in the work world—seems too efficient, too mechanical, too perfect to be human. They function more like machines than people.

Narcissists can be identified by their lack of humanness. They don't feel the tragedy of a world threatened by a nuclear holocaust, nor do they feel the tragedy of a life spent trying to prove their worth to an uncaring world. When the narcissistic façade of superiority and specialness breaks down, allowing the sense of loss and sadness to become conscious, it is often too late. One man, the head of a large company, was told that he had terminal cancer. Faced with the loss of life, he discovered what life was. "I never saw flowers before," he explained, "nor the sunshine and the fields. I spent my life trying to prove to my father that I was a success. Love had no place in my life." For the first time in his adult life, this man was able to cry and to reach out to his wife and children for help.

My theme is that narcissism denotes a degree of unreality in the individual and in the culture. Unreality is not just neurotic, it verges on the psychotic. There is something crazy about a pattern of behavior that places the achievement of success above the need to love and to be loved. There is something crazy about a person who is out of touch with the reality of his or her being—the body and its feelings. And there is something crazy about a culture that pollutes the air, the waters, and the earth in the name of a "higher" standard of living. But can a culture be insane? That idea is hardly an accepted concept in psychiatry. In general, insanity is seen as the mark of an individual who is out of touch with the reality of his or her culture. By that criterion (which has its validity), the successful narcissist is far from insane. Unless . . . unless, of course, there is some insanity in the culture. Personally, I see the frenzied activity of people in our large cities—people who are trying to make more money, gain more power, get ahead—as a little crazy. Isn't frenzy a sign of madness?

To understand the insanity that underlies narcissism, we need a broader, nontechnical view of personality problems. When we say that the noise in New York City, for example, is enough to drive one "crazy," we are speaking in a language that is real, human, and meaningful. When we describe someone as "a little crazy," we are expressing a truth not found in the psychiatric literature. I believe that psychiatry would gain much if it broadened its concepts and understanding to include the experience of people expressed in their common, everyday language.

It is my intention to share with the reader my understanding of the narcissistic condition. We need to understand the forces in the culture that create the problem and the factors in the human personality that predispose the individual to it. And we need to know what it is to be human, if we are to avoid becoming narcissists.

My treatment of narcissistic patients is directed toward

helping them get in touch with their bodies, to recover their suppressed feelings and to regain their lost humanity. This approach involves working to reduce the muscular tensions and rigidities that bind the person's feelings. But I have never regarded the specific techniques I use as the important thing. The key to therapy is understanding. Without understanding, no therapeutic approach or technique is meaningful or effective on a deep level. Only with understanding can one offer real help. All patients are desperate for someone who will understand them. As children, they were not understood by their parents; they were not seen as individuals with feelings, nor treated with respect for their humanity. No therapist who fails to see the pain in his or her patients, to sense their fear and to know the intensity of their struggle to guard their sanity in a home situation that could drive one crazy, can effectively help patients work through the narcissistic disorder.

NARCISSISM

1

A Spectrum of Narcissism

WHAT distinguishes the narcissistic disturbance? The example of a patient—Erich—may help us gain a clearer picture. It is true that Erich was somewhat unusual in that he was almost *completely* without feelings. But acting without feeling is, as we shall see, the basic disturbance in the narcissistic personality.

THE CASE OF ERICH

Erich consulted me together with his girlfriend, Janice, because their relationship was breaking up. They had lived together for a number of years, but Janice said that she could not marry him, however much she loved him, because something was lacking in their relationship. It left her dissatisfied, somehow empty. When I asked Erich what he felt, he said that he didn't understand her complaint. He tried to do what she wanted; he tried to fulfill her needs. If only she would tell him what he could do to make her happy, he would try to do it. Janice said that wasn't the problem. Something was missing in his response to her. So I asked Erich, again, what his feelings were. "Feelings!" he exclaimed. "I don't have any feelings. I don't know what you mean by feelings. I program my behavior so that it is effective in the world."

How can one explain what feeling is? It is something

that happens, not something one does. It is a bodily function, not a mental process. Erich was quite familiar with mental processes. He worked in a high-technology field, requiring knowledge of computer operations. Indeed, he saw the "programming" of his behavior as a key to his success.

I offered the example of how a man in love might feel his heart leap at the sight of his beloved. Erich countered that that was just a metaphor. So I asked him what he thought love was if it was not a bodily feeling. Love, he explained, was respect and affection for another person. Yet he was capable, he thought, of showing respect and affection, but that did not seem to be what Janice wanted. Other women, too, had complained about his inability to love, but he had never understood what they meant. I could only point out that a woman wants to sense that a man becomes excited and lights up in her presence. Love contains some ardor or passion, which is not simply respect or affection.

Erich responded by saying that he didn't want Janice to leave him. He believed they could make a good breeding team and form a workable partnership. But if she left, he didn't think he would feel any pain. Long ago, he had made himself immune to pain. As a child, he had practiced holding his breath until he didn't feel any hurt. I asked him if it would bother him if Janice went out with other men. "No," he answered. Would he be jealous? "What is jealousy?" he inquired. If there is no sense of hurt or loss when someone you love leaves you, there can be no feeling of jealousy. That feeling stems from the fear of a possible loss of love.

When Erich and Janice separated, she took her dog with her. One day Erich saw the dog on the street and felt a pain in his side. Quite seriously, he asked me, "Is that feeling?"

What had happened to turn a human being into a non-feeling machine? Theoretically, I speculated that there must have been either too much feeling or too little feeling in his childhood. When I mentioned these possibilities to Erich, he said both were true. His mother was always on the verge of hysteria; his father showed no feeling at all. As he described it, his father's coldness and hostility nearly drove his mother crazy. It was nightmarish. But Erich assured me that he was not in any distress: "My lack of feeling doesn't bother me. I get along perfectly well." The only answer I could make was: "Dead men have no pain and nothing bothers them. You have simply deadened yourself." I thought this remark would sting him. His reply amazed me. "I know I'm dead," he said.

Erich explained, "When I was young, I was terrified at the thought of death. I decided that if I were already dead, I would have nothing to fear. So I considered myself to be dead. I never thought I would reach the age of twenty. I am surprised I am still alive."

Erich's attitude to life must strike the reader as weird. He saw himself as a "thing"; he even used the word "thing" in describing his self-image. As an instrument, his purpose was to do some good for other people, although he admitted that he derived vicarious satisfaction from their responses. For example, he described himself as a very good sexual partner, capable of giving a woman much pleasure. His girlfriend added, "We have good sex, but we don't make love." Being emotionally dead, Erich derived little bodily pleasure from the sexual act. His satisfaction stemmed from the woman's response. But because of his lack of personal involvement, her climax was limited. This was something Erich could not understand. I explained that a man's orgastic response heightens and deepens a woman's excitement and brings her to a more complete orgasm. By the same token, a woman's response increases the man's excitement. Such mutuality, however, can occur only on the genital level, that is, in the act of intercourse. Erich admitted that he used his hands to bring a woman to climax because they were more sensitive than his penis. In effect, his lovemaking was more a servicing of the woman than an expression of passion. He had no passion.

Yet Erich could not be fully without feeling. If he had had absolutely no feeling, he would not have consulted me about his situation. He knew something was wrong, yet he denied any feeling about it; he knew he should change, yet he had developed powerful defenses to protect himself. One cannot attack such defenses unless one fully understands their function, and then only with the patient's cooperation. Why had Erich erected such powerful defenses against feeling? Why had he buried himself in a characterological tomb? What was he really afraid of?

I believe the answer is insanity. Erich claimed that he was afraid of death, which, I think, was true. But his fear of death was conscious, while his fear of insanity was unconscious and, therefore, deeper. I believe that the fear of death often stems from an unconscious death wish. Erich would rather have been dead than crazy. What this means is that he was closer to insanity than to death. He was convinced (albeit unconsciously) that to allow any feeling to reach consciousness would crack a hole in the dam; he would be flooded and overwhelmed by a torrent of emotion, driving him crazy. In his unconscious mind, feeling was equated with insanity and with his hysterical mother. Erich identified with his father and equated will, reason, and logic with sanity and power. He pictured himself as a "sane" person who could study a situation and react to it logically and efficiently. Logic, however, is only the application of certain principles of thought to a given premise. What is logical, therefore, depends on the premise one starts from.

I pointed out to Erich that insanity describes the state of a person who is out of touch with reality. Since feelings are a basic reality of a human life, to be out of touch with one's feelings is a sign of insanity. From this point of view, I indicated, Erich would be considered insane, despite the apparent rationality of his behavior. This suggestion that he might be crazy had a strong effect on Erich, and he asked me several questions about the nature of insanity. I explained to him that feelings are never crazy; they are always valid for the person. When, however, one cannot accept or contain one's feelings, when they seem to conflict with rational thought, one may experience oneself as split or crazy—the feelings just don't make "sense." But to deny one's feelings makes no sense either. One can do this only by dissociating the ego from the body, the foundation of one's aliveness.[1] And one has to keep up a constant effort to suppress all feeling, to act "as if." It is tiring and pointless. I compared Erich to a fugitive from justice, who dares not surrender yet who finds that the strain of hiding is unbearable. Peace can come only with surrender. If Erich could see and accept that his attitude was really insane, he would be sane. This explanation made a lot of sense to him.

What can we learn about narcissistic disturbances from Erich's case? The most important feature, I believe, is the lack of feeling. Although Erich had cut off his feelings to an extreme degree, such a lack or denial of feeling is typical of all narcissistic individuals. Another aspect of narcissism that was evident in Erich's personality was his need to project an image. He presented himself as someone committed to "doing good for others," to use his words. But this image was a perversion of reality. What he called "doing good for others" represented an exercise of power over them which, despite his stated good intentions, verged on the diabolical. Under the guise of doing good, for instance, Erich exploited his girlfriend: He got her to love him without any loving response on his part. Such exploitativeness is common to all narcissistic personalities.

A question comes up here: Can one call Erich grandiose in his exercise of power? After all, he described himself as a "thing," hardly an overblown self-image. But the "he" who observed himself, the "I" who controlled the thing, was an arrogant superpower. This arrogance of the ego is found in all narcissistic personalities, regardless of their lack of achievement or self-esteem.

A DEFINITION OF THE NARCISSIST

Through Erich, we have begun to glimpse a portrait of the narcissist. But how can we define a narcissist more precisely? In common parlance, we describe a narcissist as a person who is preoccupied with him- or herself to the exclusion of everyone else. As Theodore I. Rubin, noted psychoanalyst and writer, says, "The narcissist becomes his own world and believes the whole world is him."[2] This is certainly the broad picture. A closer view of narcissistic personalities is given by Otto Kernberg, a prominent psychoanalyst. In his words, narcissists "present various combinations of intense ambitiousness, grandiose fantasies, feelings of inferiority and overdependence on external admiration and acclaim." Also characteristic, in his opinion, are "chronic uncertainty and dissatisfaction about themselves, conscious or unconscious exploitiveness and ruthlessness toward others."[3]

But this descriptive analysis of narcissistic behavior only helps us to identify a narcissist, not to understand him or her. We need to look beneath the surface of behavior to see the underlying personality disturbance. The question is: What causes a person to be exploitative and act ruthlessly toward others and at the same time suffer from chronic uncertainty and dissatisfaction?

Psychoanalysts recognize that the problem develops in early childhood. Kernberg points to the young child's "fusion of ideal self, ideal object and actual self-images as a defense against an intolerable reality in the interpersonal realm."[4] In nontechnical language, Kernberg is saying that narcissists get hung up on their image. In effect, they cannot distinguish between an image of who they imagine themselves to be and an image of who they actually are. The two views have become one. But this statement is not yet clear enough. What happens is that the narcissist identifies with the idealized image. The actual self-image is lost. (Whether this is so because it has become fused with the idealized image, or is discarded in favor of the latter, is relatively unimportant.) Narcissists do not function in terms of the actual self-image, because it is unacceptable to them. But how can they ignore it or deny its reality? The answer is by not looking at the self. There is a difference between the self and its image, just as there is between the person and his or her reflection in a mirror.

Indeed, all this talk of "images" betrays a weakness in the psychoanalytic position. Underlying the psychoanalytic explanation of narcissistic disturbances is the belief that what goes on in the mind determines the personality. It fails to consider that what goes on in the body influences thinking and behavior as much as what goes on in the mind. Consciousness is concerned with (or even dependent on) images that regulate our actions. But we should remember that an image implies the existence of an object which it represents. The self-image—whether grandiose, idealized, or actual—must bear some relation to the self, which is *more* than an image. We need to direct our attention to the self, that is, the corporeal self, which is projected onto the mind's eye as an image. Simply put, I equate the self with the living body, which includes the mind. The sense of self depends on the perception of what goes on in the living body. Perception is a function of the mind and creates images.

If the body is the self, the actual self-image must be a bodily image. One can only discard the actual self-image by denying the reality of an *embodied* self. Narcissists don't deny that they have bodies. Their grasp of reality is not that weak. But they see the body as an instrument of the mind, subject to their will. It operates only according to their images, without feeling. Although the body can function efficiently as an instrument, perform like a machine, or impress one as a statue, it then lacks "life." And it is this feeling of aliveness that gives rise to the experience of the self.

Clearly, in my opinion, the basic disturbance in the narcissistic personality is the denial of feeling. I would define the narcissist as a person whose behavior is not motivated by feeling. But, still, we are left with the question: Why does someone choose to deny feeling? And related to this is another question: Why are narcissistic disorders so prevalent today in Western culture?

NARCISSISM VERSUS HYSTERIA

In general, the pattern of neurotic behavior at any particular time reflects the operation of cultural forces. In the Victorian period, for example, the typical neurosis was hysteria. The hysterical reaction results from the damming up of sexual excitement. It may take the form of an emotional explosion, breaking through restraining forces and overwhelming the ego. The person may then cry or scream uncontrollably. If, however, the restraining forces retain their hold, clamping down on any expression of feeling, the person may faint instead, as many Victorian women did when exposed to some public manifestation of sexuality. In other cases, the attempt to repress an early sexual experience, along with sexual feeling, may produce what is called a conversion symptom. Here the person displays some functional ailment, such as paralysis, although no physical basis for this can be found.

It was through his work with hysterical patients that Sigmund Freud began to develop psychoanalysis and his thinking on neurosis. Yet it is important to retain a picture of the society in which his observations were made. Generally speaking, Victorian culture was characterized by a rigid class structure. Sexual morality and sexual prudery were the avowed standards, with restraint and conformity the accepted attitudes. Manners of speech and dress were carefully controlled and monitored, especially in bourgeois society. Women wore tight-fitting corsets and men stiff collars. Respect for authority was the established order. The effect was to produce in many people a strict and severe superego, which limited sexual expression and created intense guilt and anxiety about sexual feeling.

Today, about a century later, the cultural picture has shifted almost 180 degrees. Our culture is marked by a breakdown of authority in and out of the home. Sexual mores seem far more easygoing. The ability of people to move from one sexual partner to another approaches their physical ability to move from one place to another. Sexual prudery has been replaced by exhibitionism and pornography. At times one wonders if there is any acceptable standard of sexual morality. In any case, one sees fewer people today who suffer from a conscious sense of guilt or anxiety about sexual feeling. Instead, many people complain about an inability to function sexually or a fear of failure in sexual performance.

Of course this is an oversimplified comparison of Victorian and modern times. Yet it can serve to underscore the contrast between the hysterical neurotics of Freud's time and the narcissistic personalities of ours. Narcissists, for instance, do not suffer from a strict, severe superego. Quite the contrary. They seem to lack what might be considered even a normal superego, providing some moral limits to sexual and other behavior. Without a sense of limits, they tend to "act out" their impulses. There is an absence of self-restraint in their responses to people and situations. Nor do they feel bound by custom or fashion. They see themselves as free to create their own life-styles, without societal rules. Again, quite the opposite of the hysterics of Freud's time.

It isn't only the behavioral picture that reveals the contrast; a similar opposition holds on the level of feeling. Hysterics are often described as oversensitive, as exaggerating their feelings. Narcissists, on the other hand, minimize their feelings, aiming to be "cool." Similarly, hysterics appear to be burdened by a sense of guilt from which narcissists seem relieved. The narcissistic predisposition is to depression, a sense of emptiness or no feeling, whereas in hysteria the predisposition is to anxiety. In hysteria there is a more or less conscious fear of being overwhelmed by feeling; in narcissism this fear is largely unconscious. But these are theoretical distinctions. Often one finds a mixture of anxiety and depression because elements of both hysteria and narcissism are present. This is especially true of the borderline personality, a variety of the narcissistic disturbance which I will discuss later in this chapter.

Let us return to our contrasting pictures of the two cultures. Victorian culture fostered strong feelings but imposed definite and heavy restraints on their expression, especially in the area of sexuality. This led to hysteria. Our present-day culture imposes relatively fewer restraints on behavior, and even encourages the "acting out" of sexual impulses in the name of liberation, but minimizes the importance of feeling. The result is narcissism. One might also say that Victorian culture emphasized love without sex, whereas our present culture emphasizes sex without love. Allowing for the fact that these statements are broad generalizations, they bring into focus the central problem of narcissism: the denial of feeling and its relation to a lack of limits. What stands out today is a tendency to regard limits as unnecessary restrictions on the human potential. Business is conducted as if there were no limit to economic growth, and even in science we encounter the idea that we can overcome death, that is, transform nature to our image. Power, performing, and productivity have become the dominant values, displacing such old-fashioned virtues as dignity, integrity, and self-respect (see Chapter 9).

IS THERE A PRIMARY NARCISSISM?

Of course, narcissism is not unique to the present age. It existed in Victorian times and throughout civilized history. Nor is the interest in narcissistic disturbances new to psychology. Already in 1914, Freud made narcissism the subject of a study. Starting from the observation that the term was originally applied to individuals who derived an erotic satisfaction from looking at their own bodies, he quickly saw that many aspects of this attitude could be found in most persons. He even thought that narcissism might be part of the "regular sexual development of human beings."[5] Originally, according to Freud, we have two sexual objects: ourselves and the person who cares for us. This belief was based on the observation that a baby can derive some erotic pleasure from his or her own body as well as from the mother's. With this in mind, Freud postulated the possible existence of "a primary narcissism in everyone which may in the long run manifest itself as dominating his object-choice."[6]

The question here is whether there is a normal stage of primary narcissism. If there is, then a pathological outcome may be viewed as the failure of the child to move from the stage of self-love (primary narcissism) to true object (other-directed) love. Implicit in this emphasis on a failure of development is the idea of a lack that blocks normal growth. To my mind, what is more important is the idea that narcissism results from a *distortion* of development. We need to look for something the parents *did* to the child rather than simply what they failed to do. Unfortunately, children are often subjected to both kinds of trauma: Parents fail to provide sufficient nurturing and support on an emotional level by not recognizing and respecting their children's individuality, but they also seductively try to mold them according to their image of how they should be. The lack of nurturing and recognition aggravates the distortion, but it is the distortion that produces the narcissistic disorder.

I don't believe in the concept of a primary narcissism. Instead, I regard all narcissism as secondary, stemming from some disturbance in the parent-child relationship. This view differs from that of most ego psychologists, who identify pathological narcissism as the result of a failure to outgrow the primary narcissistic state. Their belief in a primary narcissism rests largely on the observation that infants and young children see only themselves, that they think only of themselves and live only for themselves.

For a short time after birth, infants do seem to experience the mother as part of themselves, as she was when still in the womb. The newborn's consciousness has not developed to the point of recognizing another person's independent existence. That consciousness develops quickly, however. Infants soon show that they recognize the mother as an independent being (by smiling at her), although they still function as if the mother were there only to satisfy their needs. This expectancy on the part of the baby—that mother will always be there to respond—has been referred to as infantile omnipotence. The term, however, seems unfortunate. As the British psychoanalyst Michael Balint points out, "It is taken for granted (by the infant) that the other partner, the object on the friendly expanse, will automatically have the same wishes, interests, and expectations. This explains why this is so often called the state of omnipotence. This description is somewhat out of tune; there is no feeling of power, in fact, no need for either power or effort, as all things *are* in harmony."[7]

The issue of power, however, often enters into the relationship between parents and children. Many mothers resent the child's taking it for granted that she, the mother, will always be there to respond to the child's needs, regardless of her feelings. Children are often accused of seeking power over their parents when all they want is to have their needs understood and responded to. Infants are totally dependent and can only appeal through crying. Children are also really powerless. In fact, it is the parents who are omnipotent with respect to children, for they literally hold the power of life and death over children. Why, then, do we adults often refer to the baby as "his royal highness"? The idea of infantile omnipotence suggests a grandiosity that would justify the assumption of a primary narcissism. Yet I believe it is all in the adult mind. The parent's narcissism is projected onto the child: "I'm special and therefore my child is special."

DIFFERENT TYPES OF NARCISSISTIC DISORDER

So far we have looked at narcissism as a whole. But narcissism covers a broad spectrum of behavior; there are various degrees of disturbance or loss of self. I distinguish five different types of narcissistic disorder, according to the severity of the disorder and its special features. Thus, the differences are both quantitative and qualitative. The common element, however, is always narcissism.

In order of increasing narcissism, the five types are:

1. Phallic-Narcissistic character
2. Narcissistic character*
3. Borderline personality
4. Psychopathic personality
5. Paranoid personality

What we have, then, is a spectrum of narcissistic disorders, from least to most severe. Using this spectrum, we can see more clearly the relationships between different aspects of the narcissistic disorder. For instance, the degree to which the person identifies with his or her feelings is inversely proportional to the degree of narcissism. The more narcissistic one is, the less one is identified with one's feelings. Also, in this case, one has a greater identification with one's image (as opposed to self), along with a proportionate degree of grandiosity. In other words, there is a correlation between the denial or lack of feeling and the lack of a sense of self.

Phallic-Narcissistic Character	*Narcissistic Character*	*Borderline Personality*	*Psychopathic Personality*	*Paranoid Personality*
Lowest	←	DEGREE OF NARCISSISM	→	Highest
Lowest	←	GRANDIOSITY	→	Highest
Lowest	←	LACK OF FEELING	→	Highest
Lowest	←	LACK OF SENSE OF SELF	→	Highest
Lowest	←	LACK OF CONTACT WITH REALITY	→	Highest

Recall that I equate the self with feelings or with the sensing of the body. The relation between narcissism and the lack of a sense of self is better understood if one thinks of narcissism as egotism, as an image rather than a feeling focus.

* Although the members of all five groups can be referred to as "narcissists," some confusion may arise with the term "narcissistic character." The specification "narcissistic *character*" thus refers only to people of this particular type of narcissism.

The antithesis between the ego (a mental organization) and the self (a body/feeling entity) exists in all adults or, rather, in anyone who has developed a certain self-consciousness, which derives from the ability to form a self-image.* Because this ability is a function of the ego, narcissism is properly seen as a disturbance of ego development.

But being self-conscious or having an image of the self is not narcissistic unless the image has a measure of grandiosity. And what is grandiose can only be determined by reference to the actual self. If one has an image of oneself as attractive and appealing to the opposite sex, that image is not grandiose if one is in fact attractive and appealing. Grandiosity, and thus narcissism, is a function of the discrepancy between the image and the self. That discrepancy is at a minimum in the case of the phallic-narcissistic character, which is why that personality structure is closest to health.

The Phallic-Narcissistic Character

In its least pathological form, narcissism is the term applied to the behavior of men whose egos are invested in the seduction of women. It is these personalities who have been described as phallic-narcissistic in the psychoanalytic literature. Their narcissism consists of an inflation of and preoccupation with their sexual image. Wilhelm Reich introduced this term in 1926 to describe a character type that was somewhere between the compulsion neurosis and hysteria. "The typical phallic-narcissistic character," he writes, "is self-confident, often arrogant, elastic, vigorous and often impressive."[8]

The importance of the concept of phallic-narcissism is twofold. First, it underlines the intimate connection between narcissism and sexuality—specifically, sexuality in terms of erective potency, the symbol of which is the phallus. Second,

* The distinction between ego and self is further clarified in Chapter 2.

it describes a relatively healthy character type, in whom the narcissistic element is at a minimum. As Reich explains, even though phallic-narcissists' relationship to a loved person is more narcissistic than object-libidinal, "they often show strong attachments to people and things." Their narcissism is manifested in an "exaggerated display of self-confidence, dignity and superiority." But "in relatively unneurotic representatives of this type, social achievement, thanks to the free aggression, is strong, impulsive, energetic and usually productive."[9]

I have always considered myself a phallic-narcissistic character, and so I have some idea of how this personality type develops. I know that I was the apple of my mother's eye. She looked to me to fulfill her ambitions. I was more important to her than my father was. And although my mother was not overtly sexually seductive, the implications of her feelings were sexual. Her emotional investment in me provided an extra measure of energy and excitement to my personality. Yet her need to possess me, and thus control me, diminished my sense of self. In this situation, my ego became bigger than my self, making me a narcissistic personality. On the other hand, through my identification with my father, who was simple, hardworking, and pleasure loving, I retained my feeling for the life of the body, which is at the core of the feeling of self.

But what about the female in all this? The female counterpart to the phallic-narcissistic male is the hysterical character type.* Here I am using the term "hysteria" (from

* The term "hysterical character" was first used by Wilhelm Reich to describe a personality structure in the female that would parallel the phallic-narcissistic male,[10] and I also used this designation in my elaboration of character types in *The Language of the Body*.[11] In this character structure, as in the phallic-narcissistic male, feelings can be quite intense leading to a mixture of both hysterical and narcissistic elements in the personality. The strength of the latter deriving from a less restrictive culture prevents the buildup of repressed feeling to an explosive point.

the Greek *hystera*, or "womb") to denote the strong identification of this personality with feminine sexuality. The hysterical character is not given to overt hysterics (a symptom found in many schizophrenic personalities). It is more that she, like the phallic-narcissistic male, is preoccupied with her sexual image. She, too, is self-confident, often arrogant, vigorous, and impressive. Her narcissism comes out in a tendency to be seductive and to measure her value by her sexual appeal, based on her "feminine" charms. She is and she feels herself to be attractive to men, and she has a relatively strong sense of self. She differs from the phallic-narcissistic male in that softness is her essential quality (the softness of the womb), as opposed to his identification with the hardness of his erection. There are, of course, women who can be considered phallic in their structure and behavior. They have less feeling, sexual and otherwise, than the hysterical character and are more narcissistic, more committed to an image of superiority than to the feeling self. They belong to the narcissistic character type, which I shall describe next.

The Narcissistic Character

Narcissistic characters have a more grandiose ego image than phallic-narcissists. They are not just better, they are the best. They are not just attractive, they are the most attractive. As psychiatrist James F. Masterson points out, they have a need to be perfect and to have others see them as perfect.[12] And actually, in many cases, narcissistic characters *can* display numerous achievements and seeming success, for they often show an ability to get along in the world of power and money. They may think too highly of themselves, but others may think highly of them, too, because of their worldly success. Nevertheless, their image is grandiose; it is contradicted by the reality of the self. Narcissistic characters are completely out of place in the world of feeling and do not know how to relate to other people in a real, human way.

One way of looking at the differences between the phallic-narcissist and the narcissistic character is through their fantasies. As he walks down the street, for instance, the phallic-narcissistic male may imagine that women look at him with admiration and men with envy. On some level, he sees himself as superior, but he also recognizes that he may be inferior to others. When the narcissism is more pronounced, the fantasy might be: "When I walk down the street, I have the feeling that people step aside for me. It's like the parting of the waters of the Red Sea to allow the Hebrews to pass through. I am proud." This fantasy was in fact related by one of my patients, who said he realized it was irrational but it was how he felt. He identified himself unconsciously with those celebrities for whom the police make a corridor through the crowd of their admirers.

The Borderline Personality

The third type of narcissist—the borderline personality—may or may not overtly show the typical symptoms of narcissism. Some borderline personalities project an image of success, competence, and command in the world, which is indeed supported by achievements in the world of business or entertainment. In contrast to the front of narcissistic characters, however, this façade readily crumbles under emotional stress, and the person reveals the helpless and frightened child within. Other borderline personalities present themselves as deprived, emphasizing their vulnerability, and often clinging. In these cases, the underlying grandiosity and arrogance are hidden because they cannot be supported by proven accomplishments.

The grandiose display of narcissistic characters is a relatively effective defense against depression, and thus the façade of superiority is difficult to break down. In contrast, for borderline personalities, a show of success provides no such protection. Often these patients enter treatment with the complaint of depression. Narcissistic characters and borderline personalities may hold similar grandiose fantasies in terms of content. What differs, however, is the degree of ego strength behind these fantasies—the extent to which they are supported by a true sense of self.

The case of Richard, a borderline personality, clarifies the distinction I am making. Richard entered therapy because of depression, which was affecting both his sexual life and his work. Although he had an important job, he felt he was a failure. Perhaps, he thought, he wasn't aggressive enough. In any case, he didn't feel in command of the situation. Moreover, he was afraid of success.

There was nothing in Richard's appearance to suggest a narcissistic problem; he did not present a commanding or self-consciously handsome appearance. But something in his manner made me question his self-image. When I asked him to describe himself, he replied, "I feel I am strong, energetic, capable. I feel I am smarter and more competent than all others, and I should be recognized as such. But I hold myself back. I was born to be on top. I was born a king, superior to everyone else. I feel the same way on the sexual level. Sex should just be offered to me. Women should cater to my needs, but I act out the opposite. I hold back."

The idea of being "born a king," of being extremely special, certainly dovetails with the fantasies of the narcissistic character. But Richard repeatedly excuses himself, saying: "I hold back." In contrast, narcissistic characters do *not* hold back. They have the necessary aggression to achieve some degree of success, suggesting an ego strength that the borderline personality lacks. One should not, however, underestimate the grandiosity of the borderline. Though seemingly less evident than in the narcissistic character, it is no less present, as another example shows.

Carol had been in therapy for several years with complaints of depression and feelings of worthlessness. That such feelings may cover underlying feelings of superiority should not be surprising. We have known for a long time that feelings of superiority and inferiority exist together. If one is on top, the other is underneath.

In describing herself to me, Carol commented: "I was a superior student at college. I always got the highest marks. And I did equally well in graduate school. I was considered the top student and congratulated on my abilities. My professors raved about me. They told me I was exceptional. I thought I was great. However, in my work now I often sense that I do not know what to do. I feel awful about myself. It was the same at home when I was young. I was great one minute and shit the next. My mother would say I was the most beautiful, the most brilliant child. The next day she said it wasn't true, she had said it just to bolster me up because I was so pathetic. She built me up one minute, then smashed me down the next."

Carol's remarks point out one difference between narcissistic characters and borderline personalities. Although the narcissistic character's self-image is grandiose, it is in less direct conflict with realitv for it has never truly been smashed down. In contrast, borderline personalities find themselves caught between two contradictory views—they are either totally great or totally worthless. The fantasy of "secret" greatness may then become all the more necessary, to counter the reality threat of worthlessness. There is thus less connection between the inner (fantasy) image and the actual self, however deprecatory the patient's comments may sound.

Still, I must emphasize that the differences between the various narcissistic types are largely a matter of degree. Some borderline patients, despite their feelings of inferiority and insecurity, attain a fair measure of success in their work. And some narcissistic characters are troubled by a sense of inadequacy despite their façade of self-assurance and command.

In these cases, one may be uncertain about the exact diagnosis. Granted, an exact diagnosis is not necessary to begin treatment, for one should treat the individual, not the symptom. Nevertheless, diagnosis can help us to better understand the underlying personality disturbance. With the diagnosis of narcissistic character disorder, for instance, we would expect the patient to have a better developed ego and sense of self than the borderline personality, so our emphasis might be slightly different in the treatment.

This distinction poses a theoretical problem for many psychoanalytic writers on the subject who see narcissism as resulting from the failure of ego development. As Masterson explains, "in developmental terms, although the self-object representation is fused, the narcissistic [character] seems to get the benefit for ego development that is believed to come about only as a result of separation from that fusion."[13] To these writers, grandiosity represents a continuation of infantile omnipotence, which stems from the child's failure to form an identity separate from that of the primary love object, the mother. The fusion of self and object representations is characteristic of the infantile state. The problem can be rephrased as follows: If, on an emotional level, the narcissistic character is still an infant tied to mother, how can we explain his or her possession of an aggression that is oriented to the world and leads to achievements beyond the capacity of the borderline personality?

I don't believe this problem can be resolved if we rely on the premise of infantile omnipotence and regard narcissism *only* as the result of a failure of development. If we drop the concept of infantile omnipotence, then we may seek the cause for grandiosity in the parents' relation to the child, rather than in the child's relation to the parents. A boy doesn't think himself a prince through any failure of normal development. If he believes himself to be a prince, it is because he was raised in that belief. How children see themselves often reflects how their parents saw and treated them.

The Psychopathic Personality

Moving along our spectrum to the psychopathic personality, we would expect to find an even greater degree of grandiosity, whether manifest or latent. All psychopathic personalities consider themselves superior to other people and show a degree of arrogance that verges on contempt for common humanity. Like other narcissists, they deny their feelings. Particularly characteristic of psychopathic personalities is a tendency to act out, often in an antisocial way. They will lie, cheat, steal, even kill, without any sign of guilt or remorse. This extreme lack of human fellow-feeling makes psychopathic personalities very difficult to treat.

The term "acting out" describes an impulsive type of behavior that ignores the feelings of other persons and is generally destructive to the best interests of the self. The impulses underlying this behavior stem from experiences in early childhood that were so traumatic and so overwhelming that they could not be integrated into the developing ego. As a result, the feelings associated with these impulses are beyond the ego's perception. The action is therefore taken without any conscious feeling. Murder in cold blood is an extreme example of psychopathic acting out. But acting out per se is not limited to antisocial behavior. Alcoholism, drug addiction, and promiscuous sexual behavior may all be regarded as forms of acting out.

Acting out, however, is not limited to the psychopathic personality. Masterson recognizes that narcissistic characters and borderline personalities also act out. But there is a difference. As he puts it, "The acting out of the psychopath, compared to that of the borderline or narcissistic [character] disorders, is more commonly antisocial and usually of long duration."[14] Here, again, we see that the differences are a matter of degree rather than of kind.

Because psychopathic personalities represent an extreme,

they provide many insights into the nature of narcissism. Not only do they portray in sharp relief narcissists' tendency to act out (which, in other cases, is less antisocial), but they also shed light on narcissists' underlying grandiosity. It is significant, for instance, that narcissistic characters and psychopathic personalities show a need for instant gratification, an inability to contain desire or tolerate frustration. One could regard this weakness as an expression of infantilism in the personality, but I believe it has a different meaning and origin, reflecting the deficient sense of self. One must remember that in other respects—namely, in their ability to manipulate people, organize and promote schemes, and attract followers—narcissistic characters and psychopathic personalities are anything but infantile.

In saying this, I should add that psychopathic personalities are not necessarily what society calls "losers." There are successful psychopaths according to Alan Harrington, who made a study of these personalities—"brilliant, remorseless people with icy intelligence, incapable of love or guilt, with aggressive designs on the rest of the world."[15] Such an individual may be an able lawyer, executive, or politician. "Instead of murdering others," Harrington comments, this person "might become a corporate raider and murder companies, firing people instead of killing them, and chopping up their functions, rather than their bodies."[16] Ironically, the key to this kind of "success" is the person's lack of feeling —which is the key to all narcissistic disturbances. As we have seen, the greater the denial of feeling, the more narcissistically disturbed the individual is.

The Paranoid Personality

At the other end of the spectrum, furthest removed from health, is the paranoid personality showing clear-cut megalomania. Paranoid personalities believe that people are not only looking at them but also talking about them, even conspiring against them, because they are very special and very important. They may believe they have extraordinary powers. When they become unable to distinguish fantasy from fact, their insanity is clear. In that case, we are dealing with full-fledged paranoia—a psychotic rather than a neurotic condition—and the treatment differs. Nevertheless, even in such extreme cases, we find most of the characteristics of narcissism: extreme grandiosity, a marked discrepancy between the ego image and the actual self, arrogance, insensitivity to others, denial, and projection.

Just as it may be difficult to distinguish between the narcissistic disturbances on our spectrum, it may at times be hard to draw a sharp line between neurosis and psychosis. The very term "borderline" was created to denote a personality structure that is somewhere in between, both sane and insane. If sanity is measured by the congruence of one's ego image with the reality of the self or body,[17] then we may postulate that there is a degree of insanity in every narcissistic disturbance. To return to the beginning, Erich's self-representation as a "thing" denotes a degree of unreality that borders on the insane.

2

The Role of the Image

ORDINARILY we think of narcissism as an inordinate love of the self, with a corresponding lack of interest and feeling for other people. The narcissist is depicted as selfish and greedy, as someone whose attitude is "me first," and in most cases, "me only." But this picture is only partially correct. Narcissists do show a lack of concern for others, but they are equally insensitive to their own true needs. Often their behavior is self-destructive. Moreover, when we speak of narcissists' "self" love, we need to make a distinction. Narcissism denotes an investment in one's image as opposed to one's self. Narcissists love their image, not their real self. They have a poor sense of self; they are not self-directed. Instead, their activities are directed toward the enhancement of their image, often at the expense of the self.

But aren't we all concerned about our image, and don't we invest a lot of energy trying to improve it? Many of us spend considerable time and money selecting clothes that will create the kind of image we wish to project. We believe that appearance is important, and we often go to great lengths to present a favorable appearance. We want to look younger, more beautiful, more virile, more chic, etc. Some people even resort to plastic surgery to achieve these ends. This preoccupation with appearance is so much a part of our way of living that we may regard a person who neglects his or her appearance as being emotionally disturbed.

Are we all narcissistic, then? Does it mean that narcissism is a normal aspect of the human personality? No. In my opinion, narcissism is a pathological condition. I draw a distinction between a healthy concern for one's appearance, based on a sense of self, and the displacement of identity from the self to the image, which is characteristic of the narcissistic state. This view of narcissism is in line with the Narcissus myth.

THE MYTH OF NARCISSUS

According to the Greek myth, Narcissus was a handsome young Thespian with whom the nymph Echo fell in love. Echo had been deprived of speech by Hera, the wife of Zeus, and could only repeat the last syllables of words she heard. Unable to express her love for Narcissus, she was spurned by him and died of a broken heart. The gods then punished Narcissus for his callous treatment of Echo by making him fall in love with his own image. It had been predicted by the seer Tiresias that Narcissus would live until he saw himself. One day while he was leaning over the limpid waters of a fountain, Narcissus caught sight of his own reflection in the water. He became passionately enamored of his image and refused to leave the spot. He died of languor and turned into a flower—the narcissus that grows at the edges of springs.

It is significant that Narcissus fell in love with his image only after he rejected the love of Echo. Falling in love with one's image—that is, becoming narcissistic—is seen in the myth as a form of punishment for being incapable of loving. But let's take the legend one step further. Who is Echo? She could be our own voice coming back to ourselves. Thus, if Narcissus could say "I love you," Echo would repeat these words and Narcissus would feel loved. The inability to say those words identifies the narcissist. Having withdrawn their libido from people in the world, narcissists are condemned to fall in love with their image—that is, direct their libido to their ego.

Another possible interpretation is interesting. In rejecting Echo, Narcissus also rejected his own voice. Now, the voice is the expression of one's inner being, one's bodily self as opposed to one's surface appearance. The quality of the voice is determined by the resonance of the air in the inner passages and chambers. The word "personality" reflects this idea. *Persona* means that by his or her sound you can know the person. According to this interpretation, Narcissus denied his inner being in favor of his appearance. And that is a typical maneuver of narcissists.

What is the importance of the prophecy uttered by the seer Tiresias—that Narcissus would die when he saw himself? What grounds could there be for such a prediction? I believe it had to be the exceptional beauty of Narcissus. Such beauty in either a man or woman often proves to be more of a curse than a blessing. One danger is that the awareness of such beauty will go to the person's head, making him or her an egotist. Another possibility is that this beauty will arouse violent passions of desire and envy in others, leading to tragedy. History and fiction contain many tales of the unhappy endings to the lives of beautiful people. The story of Cleopatra is one of the best known. A seer, being a wise person, understands these dangers.

AUTOEROTICISM AND NARCISSISM

Let us now look again at the psychiatric history of the term "narcissism." It was originally introduced to explain the behavior of people who derived an erotic excitation from looking at, caressing, and fondling their own bodies. Such behavior was considered a perversion. As we saw in Chapter 1, however, Freud recognized that some aspects of this attitude could be found in other disorders and perhaps even in normal people. In developing his thinking on narcissism, Freud characterized schizophrenia as entailing an equal loss of libidinal interest in people and things in the external world. He, then, distinguished schizophrenia from obsessional neuroses and hysteria, in which there is also a disturbed relationship to sexual objects. The difference, according to Freud, is that in the neuroses, sexual interest (or libido) is still attached to the object in the form of fantasy, although the motor activities needed to establish a real relationship are blocked. In schizophrenia, on the other hand, the libido is withdrawn from the object or its image and focused on the self-image, producing megalomania. In Freud's words: "The libido withdrawn from the outer world has been diverted onto the ego, giving rise to a state we may call narcissism."[1]

A question arose in Freud's mind, as it must in ours: What is the difference between the narcissistic perversion and autoerotic activities such as masturbation? No one would characterize masturbation as narcissistic, although sexual satisfaction is derived from fondling one's own body. The difference is that in masturbation the body is recognized as the self. In a perversion, however, one sees one's body as a sexual object—that is, as another person. One is not identified with one's body, but rather dissociated from it. Narcissus, for instance, was not in love with himself but with his image, which took on an independent reality. Simply put, autoerotic activities are a manifestation of self-love, whereas narcissism is a form of image or ego love.

SELF AND EGO

But what exactly do I mean by self-love in contrast to a narcissistic preoccupation? To understand this, we need to clarify the concept of self. I believe that an infant is born with a self, which is a biological, not a psychological, phenomenon. The ego, in contrast, is a mental organization that develops as the child grows. The sense of self or the consciousness of self comes into being as the ego (the mental "I") becomes defined through self-awareness, self-expression, and self-possession. But these terms refer to feeling—to the awareness of, the expression of, and the containment of feeling. The self, then, may be defined as the feeling aspect of the body. It can be experienced only as a feeling. One might say: "I feel myself as angry, as sad, as hungry, as sleepy," etc. More simply, of course, one says: "I am angry, sad, hungry, sleepy," etc. Indeed, emphasizing the feeling in this way makes the statement an expression of the self. If the emphasis is placed upon the "I," it becomes an ego statement.

We must avoid confusing or identifying the ego with the self. The ego is not the self, though it is that part of the personality that perceives the self. Actually, the ego represents self-consciousness, or consciousness of self: I (ego) feel (perceive) myself to be angry. Descartes was right when he said: "I think, therefore I am" (with the emphasis on the *I*). He would be wrong if he believed that thinking determined the self. Computers may be said to think; what they cannot do is feel.

By dissociating the ego from the body or self, narcissists sever consciousness from its living foundation. Instead of functioning as an integrated whole, the personality is split into two parts: an active, observing "I" (the ego), with which the individual identifies, and a passive, observed object (the body). It is true that the ego is concerned with perception of the inner state of the organism and the other state of the world, and helps to adapt one to the other to promote the welfare of the self. One function of the ego, for instance, is to control the action of the voluntary musculature through the will, thus regulating the person's conscious response to the world. But, again, the ego is *not* the self—only the conscious aspect of the self. Nor is it separate from the self. The accuracy of its perception depends on its connection, as part of the self.

The greater part of the self consists of the body and its functions, most of which operate below the level of consciousness. The unconscious is like the submerged part of an iceberg. Involuntary functions like circulation, digestion, and respiration have a profound effect on consciousness, for they determine the organism's state of being. Depending on the body's functioning, one may feel well or sick, in good spirits or downhearted, vital and alive or depressed, sexually excited or impotent. What we feel depends on what happens in the body. The will or ego is incapable of creating a feeling, although it may try to control the feeling. One can't truly will a sexual response, an appetite, a feeling of love, or even anger—however much one may "think" one can. Images may focus these feelings in consciousness, provided they are already present in the body as potential events. For body happenings to lead to the perception of feeling, the events must reach the surface of the body and the surface of the mind, where consciousness is located. Only that part of the iceberg that lies at or above the surface of the water is visible.

We have a dual relationship to our bodies. We can experience the body directly through feeling or we can have an image of it. In the first case, we are immediately connected to the self, whereas in the second case, the connection is indirect. A healthy person has this dual consciousness, but it does not pose a problem because the self-image and the direct self-experience through the body coincide. What such a state presupposes is self-acceptance—an acceptance of and identification with the body and its feelings. It is self-acceptance that is lacking in narcissistic individuals, who have dissociated their bodies, so that libido is invested in the ego and not in the body or the self. Without self-acceptance, there is no self-love.

I have long maintained that if one does not love oneself, one cannot love others. Love may be viewed as a sharing of the self with another person. Sexual intercourse is a true expression of love when there is such a sharing but a narcissistic act when it is lacking. Intimacy describes the sharing of the self. But one has to have a sense of self in order to share it. Although we are born with a self, we can lose a sense of self if we turn against the self, if we invest our energies (Freud's libido) in the ego or self-image. All of us need others. If we have a sense of self, we need another person to share it. But even if we lack a sense of self, like the narcissist, we still need others—to support and applaud our self-image. Without the approval and admiration of others, the narcissistic ego becomes deflated, for it is not connected to and nourished by self-love. On the other hand, the admiration the narcissist receives only inflates his or her ego; it does nothing for the self. In the end, then, the narcissist will reject admirers, just as he or she has rejected the true self.

The relation between the ego and the self is complex. Without an ego, there can be no sense of self. But without a felt self, the sense of identity becomes attached to the "I." Actually, the human being has a dual identity—one part deriving from identification with the ego, the other from identification with the body and its feelings. From the ego's point of view, the body is an object to be observed, studied, and controlled in the interest of a performance that measures up to one's image. On this level, identity is represented by the "I" in its functions of conscious perception, thinking, and action. Again, it is from this perspective that we can correctly say: "I think, therefore I am." And we might add: "I will, therefore I am"—for will is an important aspect of the ego.

But what about the other view? We are moved by our feelings as well as by our will—at least, if we haven't denied our feelings. We are moved to tears or anger or any other emotion, and our sense of being is identified with the feeling. Again, saying "I am sad" or "I am angry" expresses the idea that we are what we feel. In this case, it is the body that plays the active role, informing the mind of its needs and desires and determining the direction and aim of the person's actions.

Of course, both positions are valid: We both think and feel. Our dual identity rests on our ability to form a self-image and on our awareness of the bodily self. In a healthy person, the two identities are congruent. The image fits the body reality as a glove fits its owner's hand. A personality disturbance occurs when there is a lack of congruence between the self-image and the self. The severity of this disturbance is in direct proportion to the degree of incongruence. The discrepancy is most marked in schizophrenia, where the image bears almost no relationship to reality. Mental institutions contain many people who see themselves as Jesus Christ, Napoleon, or some other renowned figure. Since this image conflicts sharply with the bodily reality, the result is confusion. The schizophrenic attempts to undo this confusion by dissociating the reality of his or her body, which leads to a withdrawal from reality in general. In narcissistic disorders, the incongruence is less than in schizophrenia, but it is sufficient to produce a split in identity, with resulting confusion. Narcissists avoid the confusion by denying the identity based on their bodies without, however, dissociating their bodies. By focusing their attention and interest solely on the image, they can ignore the bodily self. By not allowing any strong feelings to reach consciousness, they can treat the body as an object subject to the control of their will. Yet by remaining conscious of the body, they remain oriented in time and space.

Recall Freud's statement that in narcissism libido is withdrawn from objects in the world and directed onto the ego. We might add that libido is withdrawn from the body and invested in the ego. In effect, the two statements are identical, for we experience the external world only through the body. If we deny feeling to the body, we cut off our feeling relationship to the world.

The investment of libido or energy in the ego or the image is often a deliberate undertaking. People engage in many activities designed primarily to enhance their image. Gaining power and making money, for instance, often have little to do with feelings on the body level. The ego satisfaction they provide stems from their support of one's image. Having a book published, for example, can do great things for one's ego. One can base one's identity on being an author. But it does nothing for one's body and little for one's sense of self based on the body. If one's ego becomes inflated by success or achievement, congruence with the reality of one's body is lost. Confusion can be avoided, then, only by denying one's body and its feelings. It makes little difference if the achievement is in the public interest if its effect is to produce an overinflation of the ego. People may have a public image based on their social position and power, but this does not make them narcissists. They do become narcissistic, however, if they base their personal identity on this public image rather than on their body feelings.

IMAGE AND BODY

It is a sign of the narcissistic tendency of our culture that people have become overinvolved with their images. The current preoccupation with the body partly reflects this narcissistic attitude, as Christopher Lasch has pointed out.[2] Yet, in part, it also reflects a concern for health. I strongly believe we need to be aware of our bodies and to engage in physical activities that will increase our vitality and aliveness. For too many people, however, the goal of exercise programs is to *look* (not feel) good, in accord with the current fashion ideal. They want a lean, tight, hard body, capable of performing with machinelike efficiency at the command of the will. Or they may aim for a statuesque quality, for the body of a young Adonis or Venus. An extreme example is body building through the use of weights, which produces massive, overdeveloped muscles. In my opinion, it is a narcissistic enterprise that is harmful to mental and physical health. The heavy musculature may make one look strong, but it reduces the body's spontaneity and aliveness and seriously restricts breathing.

Some indication of the current narcissistic devotion to fashion comes out in the title of a recent book on exercise and physical fitness: *Don't Be Fat—Be Flat.* The flatness refers to a flat abdomen—that is, no belly. But to really achieve this, one would have to tense the abdominal muscles to the point where abdominal respiration (a normal and healthy phenomenon) was almost impossible. And quite aside from its adverse effect on health, flatness is a negative quality from the point of view of looks and taste. Describing something as "flat" denotes that it is without taste or appeal. To "flatten" someone is to demolish him or her. And in psychological terms, "flatness" of affect describes a lack of feeling. But, of course, in those terms we can appreciate why flatness may be viewed as a virtue by narcissists.

None of this denies the value of looking good when it is an expression of a good feeling in one's body. In that case, looking good is manifested in bright eyes, glowing skin, a soft and pleasant facial expression, and a body that is vibrantly alive and graceful in its movements. Without a good body feeling, a person can only project an image of what he or she thinks a good-looking body should be. The more one focuses on this image, the more one is deprived of good feelings in one's body. In the end, the image proves a poor mask; it no longer hides the tragedy of the empty life within.

The Case of Ann

Recently, I worked with a young woman named Ann who had a constant smile on her face to show the world how happy and content she was. Yet this expression was belied by a tight, square jaw and a flat forehead, which gave her face a grim look. Ann was unaware of this contradiction. She was identified with the smiling, happy image, and she saw herself as a person who was responsible, considerate, and helpful.

When I inquired into Ann's background, she said that she was the oldest of three children. She had always been a "good" girl, doing what was expected of her and taking care of her younger siblings. After she grew up, she continued this pattern of behavior—it had become second nature to her. Yet on some deep level, it left her dissatisfied and unfulfilled. Ann was thus not entirely surprised when I pointed out the grimness of her set jaw and forehead. She agreed when I suggested that while she did a lot for others, she asked very little for herself.

Ann's smile was a façade erected to hide her unhappiness from the world and from herself. The image of the happy young woman bore little relationship to the reality of her being or her feelings. How did that image arise? Ann mentioned that her father used to tell her to put on a happy face regardless of how she felt. No one would love a sad-looking person. So Ann denied her feelings and adopted an image that would be acceptable to her father. In the process, she had to sacrifice her true self.

Ann's case shows how an image can be misused, how it can serve to replace an unacceptable self with an acceptable, even admired, façade. This substitution occurs in childhood, under pressure from the parents that leaves the child no choice. But once the substitution is made, the image becomes all-important. The person now admires the image he or she projects and, like Narcissus, falls in love with it. This love is not self-love, for with the façade the person has rejected the true self as unacceptable.

The Story of Dorian Gray

Oscar Wilde's *The Picture of Dorian Gray* is a classic study of the narcissistic personality, even if it is a fictional account. Like Narcissus, Dorian Gray was an exceedingly beautiful young man. Moreover, the beauty of his appearance coincided with an equal beauty of temperament. He was kind, considerate, and concerned. Inevitably, Dorian's good looks attracted the interest of a well-known artist, who undertook to paint his portrait. They also excited the interest of a dilettante, Lord Henry, who undertook to teach him the ways of the sophisticated world.

With appropriate flattery, Lord Henry seduced Dorian Gray into thinking he was special because of his exceptional physical beauty. Lord Henry convinced the young man that it was his duty to preserve his good looks. One way to do that was not to allow any strong feeling to disturb the placidity of his mind or mark the surface of his body. But how can one prevent the ravages of time? Dorian became preoccupied with and worried about his appearance. What a shame, he thought, that the picture should always show him as a happy, radiant, and beautiful young man, while he himself aged and deteriorated. Would that it were the reverse, he prayed, and so it came to be.

Dorian Gray passed the years without showing any sign

of age or trouble in his face and body. At fifty he looked as he had at twenty. No line or wrinkle reflecting the cares and concerns of living marred his visage. His secret was the picture, which aged and showed the ugliness of a life lived without feeling. But Dorian hid the picture and never looked at it.

In the absence of feeling, Dorian Gray spent his life seeking sensation. He seduced women (which was very easy to do with his charm and good looks), then abandoned them. He introduced the young men who admired him to vices and drugs, which ruined their lives. Very early in his career, he brought about the suicide of a lovely young actress, who fell in love with him but whom he rejected when her acting failed to measure up to the star performances that had initially attracted him to her. Throughout all this, Dorian felt no remorse. He never looked at the picture; he never confronted the reality of his life.

Besides Dorian Gray, no one knew of the picture except the painter and Lord Henry. When the painter demanded to see the picture, Dorian killed him. To hide his crime, he blackmailed a former admirer into disposing of the body. This person then committed suicide. Finally, however, Dorian could no longer restrain his curiosity about the picture, nor still the growing inner torment. Venturing into the hiding place, he removed the covering from the picture. The twisted, tortured look on the aged face struck him with such horror that he took a knife and slashed the picture. The next morning, a servant discovered him lying in front of the picture, with a knife in his heart—an old man with a twisted, tortured face.

How could such a beautiful young man become such an ugly character? Initially, Dorian Gray's beauty was not skin-deep; it was not a façade. At first he was as good inwardly as he was good-looking outwardly. But Oscar Wilde believed that human nature is corruptible, and I would agree with him. The innocent can be seduced by the promise of power or love or wealth or position. This seduction goes on all the time in our culture, fostering the development of narcissistic personalities.

Though the story of Dorian Gray is fiction, the idea that a person can present a physical appearance that belies the inner state of his being is valid. I have been struck by how many narcissistic individuals look much younger than they are. They have even features and smooth complexions, which do not show any lines of worry or trouble. These people do not allow life to touch them—specifically, they don't allow the inner events of living to reach the surface of their minds or the surface of their bodies. This constitutes a denial of feeling. But human beings are not immune to life, and in these cases, the aging occurs internally. Finally, as in Dorian Gray's case, the pain and ugliness break through the denial, and the person seems to age overnight.

To some degree, however, we are all like Dorian Gray. Often we are surprised, even shocked, when we examine our faces in a mirror. We are stunned by the lines of age we see, by the sadness in our eyes, by the pain in our expression. We did not expect to see ourselves like that. In the mind's eye, we saw ourselves as young, with smooth skin and a carefree expression. Like Dorian Gray, we don't want to face the reality of our lives. This discrepancy between the way we look and the way we see ourselves also extends to the body, which should be more visible to us than the face. We close our eyes to the lack of harmony in our body parts and the lack of grace in our movements. Clothes help us hide this reality from ourselves and others and allow us to form a picture of our bodies that is far removed from reality.

Very early we are taught to cover up our feelings and put on a face for the world. The lesson I was given as a child was: "Smile and the world smiles with you, cry and you cry alone." We saw how Ann was made to put on a "happy" face. Ellen told me a similar story: "I have a memory of sitting coyly while my picture was being taken. I still have the photo. The image is: 'See what a lovely little girl I am.' My father used to say: 'All a girl has to do is smile and she can have anything she wants.' So I went through life smiling while my heart was breaking inside."

In many cases, the body as well as the face is mobilized to project an image. The wish to appear youthful often requires that the body be rigorously disciplined through exercise and diet to retain a lean, thin look. Or if the image is one of strength and virility, a man may seek to expand his chest and build his muscles to achieve the appropriate look.

The Case of Mary

I was consulted by a woman, Mary, who had had a breakdown after a threatened breakup with her lover. She was very attractive looking—her face was well formed, with a strong jaw, a full mouth, and widely spaced eyes; her body was rather petite, very trim, with shapely legs. Her smile was warm and inviting. At least this was my impression when she directed her attention to me. When she looked away and was quiet, however, a pathetic look crept onto her face. The same pathetic quality was apparent in her body. Her chest seemed narrow and tight, her waist so constricted that it almost divided her in half. Somehow, she had no belly and her pelvis was surprisingly small, given that she had had two children (in an earlier marriage). Her body looked so tiny and undercharged that I thought, "No body. She is a nobody."

The idea that Mary could be considered a nobody was contradicted by her seeming command of her movements, her ideas, and her words. Her will was strong, and she knew how to use herself. From the age of five, she had trained to be a ballet dancer, and although she had never danced professionally, she considered herself a dancer. Knowing this, I realized that when she turned on her charm as she looked at me, it was a performance. She became a vivacious, dancing doll; indeed, her body and her face had a doll-like quality. This was the image with which she was identified and which she tried to project. When she dropped her act and looked away, she became a pathetic, lost creature, a nobody. The role of the image was to compensate for a diminished sense of self, but its effect was the reverse. By directing all her energies to maintain an image, Mary impoverished and diminished her real self.

Even though Mary recognized the weakness in her sense of self (she got depressed easily, she was overwhelmed by any strong feeling), she was not prepared to give up her image. She sensed the power in it—a power over men. Though she was past thirty-five, Mary portrayed herself as more a girl than a woman. What men were attracted to, and even fell deeply in love with, was a cute, dancing doll-girl who was openly seductive. After a relationship developed, Mary became completely dependent on the man. She oscillated between the pathetic little girl, who needed to be cared for and protected, and the seductive, dancing doll, whom men wanted to possess.

If we ask what is the reality of Mary's personality, we must answer that the image of the dancing doll is as real as the image of the pathetic little girl. In effect, Mary has a double personality in the sense that she presents two different faces to the world. One face is a mask like a doll's face that is devoid of feeling. The other face expresses her true feelings and is therefore a true representation of the self. The doll's face reflects an ego image and the pathetic little girl's face reflects the self-image. One face is put on by an effort of the will, while the other is a spontaneous manifestation of the inner being. This splitting of Mary's personality would justify the diagnosis of borderline condition.

Although diagnostically Mary would be seen as a borderline personality, in my opinion, the diagnosis is less important than understanding Mary—who she is, who she pretends to be, and why she developed a split in her personality. The image is really a part of the self. It is the part of the self that faces the world, and it takes its shape through the surface aspects of the body (posture, movement, facial expression, etc.). Because this part of the body is subject to conscious control by the will or ego, it can be modified to conform to a particular image. We can speak of a false self set up against the true self, but I prefer to describe the split in terms of an image that contradicts the self, and to see the basic disturbance as a conflict between the image and the bodily self.

Why did Mary give up her bodily self in favor of an image? Although the sacrifice was not conscious, she had decided her feeling self was not acceptable. I found that she couldn't cry and couldn't scream. She had no voice to express feelings. Her speaking voice sounded flat, unemotional, and mechanical. It was clear why Mary became a dancer. Unable to use her voice to express herself, she turned to movement. But that avenue, too, was circumscribed. She began to study ballet at five years of age with the support and encouragement of her mother, who wanted Mary to be outstanding and bring some credit to her. Mary was completely dominated by her mother and terrified of her. Yet she insisted to me that she had no angry feelings toward her mother, who had done so much for her. The degree of denial in this statement is typical of narcissists. Having accepted and identified with the image of the dancing doll which she saw as being special and superior, she couldn't admit to "bad" or angry feelings which would contradict this image.

Her father adored his little dancing doll, but his adoration was coupled with a sexual interest in her. At an early age, Mary was aware of her ability to excite her father, but any sexual feeling on her part had to be denied to avoid her mother's jealousy and her father's negative reaction (from guilt). She mentioned that when she was a teenager, her father would become very upset if he saw her kissing a boy. Without any support from her father for her feelings, Mary surrendered herself to her mother and identified with her in contempt for her weak father. Having made the surrender, she could compensate for the loss by creating an image that gave her sexual power over men without the vulnerability engendered by sexual feelings. Images can only be deflated, not hurt.

In a borderline personality, such as Mary, the discrepancy between the image and the bodily or feeling self is wide enough to pose a danger of emotional breakdown. Mary had been hospitalized before consulting me. Fortunately, I was able to help Mary get in touch with and release some of her sadness by crying. This enabled her to break through the denial, see the reality of her being, and make a connection to her bodily self which gave her a strength she had not previously possessed.

In my therapeutic approach called bioenergetic analysis, the individual's connection to his or her bodily self is achieved through direct work with the body. Special exercises are used to help a person feel those areas of the body in which chronic muscular tensions block the awareness and expression of feeling. Thus, in Mary's case, one of the exercises used was to have her lie on a bed and kick with her legs while loudly yelling "no." She had never been able to protest the surrender of her bodily self, and she could not reclaim that self until she had voiced that protest. Despite the fact that she was a dancer, her kicking movements were uncoordinated and without force while her voice was small and weak. She felt the constriction in her throat which prevented her from making a loud, full sound. It also restricted her breathing, which decreased her metabolism and lowered her energy. I could palpate the constriction as a spasticity of the scalene muscles on the sides of her neck. The technique I use to reduce this spasticity is to apply a light pressure with the tips of my fingers to these muscles while the person is making as high-pitched a sound as possible. When I did this with Mary, she broke into a loud scream which continued for some time. After several screams, she broke into a deep sobbing as the tension in the muscles of her neck relaxed and the feeling of sadness broke through. Following this release, her protests by kicking and yelling were stronger and more forceful.

People in trouble need to cry. While it was relatively easy to get Mary to cry because her body was not heavily armored, one faces considerable difficulty with narcissistic men who pride themselves on being able to take it without breaking down. The muscular overdevelopment results in a tight, hard body which effectively inhibits the awareness and expression of soft or tender feelings. In such cases, it often takes considerable work with breathing to soften the body to the point where crying can occur. Once the person lets himself cry, it is not too difficult to evoke the anger which has been suppressed. Sometimes, releasing the anger by having a person hit the bed with a tennis racket or the fists may open the sadness and produce the crying. I have described some of the exercises and body techniques in my previous books. I must emphasize that these exercises are not mechanical. They are effective in changing personality only when they are coupled with a thorough analysis, including the interpretation of dreams, and when they follow from an understanding of the personality as it is expressed by the body.

In other patients, such as narcissistic characters, the ego is able to maintain control and avoid a breakdown because it is less completely split off from the self. Yet props, like alcohol, may be used to maintain a certain denial of reality, as can be seen in Arthur's case.

The Case of Arthur

Arthur had been a well-known and successful actor. In the past two years, however, he had become subject to increasing fits of despair, which prevented him from working.

He admitted that he had begun to drink heavily. As a result, his professional standing had slipped, and he was finding it difficult to obtain parts. He also complained about his in ability to establish a satisfactory relationship with a woman. He mentioned that he had once had a short-lived experience of deep love, and it had made him feel good and fulfilled. He desperately wanted to feel that way again.

It should not come as a surprise to find a narcissist engaged in acting as a profession. Acting depends on an ability to project an image. This comes easily to the narcissistic individual, who is acting all the time—although, of course, not all actors are narcissists.

As Arthur stood before me, his bodily attitude was one of hauteur and superiority. He was well built, with a rather handsome, dramatic face. When he drew himself up and turned his charm on, he appeared imposing. His eyes, as they regarded me, had an intense expression—as if he were trying to magnetize me. I could feel the power of his look. Yet because this look required an effort, sapping all his energy, he could not maintain it. When the effort collapsed, his face looked tense and tired. Part of Arthur's charm was a seemingly innocent smile, which he gave me from time to time. But I could see that it covered an intense fear. Most striking, however, were the different expressions on the two halves of his face. His right eyebrow was strongly arched upward in a supercilious expression; the left eyebrow was flattened and pulled downward. As a result, his face had a twisted look. When I mentioned this observation to him, he said that he was aware of it. He was also aware that his face had a very pained expression. He had studied his face in a mirror, but in typical narcissistic fashion, he did not allow himself to feel any pain or fear.

The split in Arthur's personality was quite evident. From his face I had the impression that his right side was struggling desperately to rise above and deny the despair evident on the left side. One part of him was identified with an image of superiority, which he tried to project to cover over and compensate for an inner feeling of inferiority. He needed an image of power to overcome an inner sense of helplessness and powerlessness.

Like Dorian Gray, Arthur had had his days of power and glory. When he was younger and a matinee idol, many women were attracted to him. He had the energy then to sustain the image against any inner doubts. But the rewards success provides do not nourish the self. The admiration and acclaim of the crowd only feed the ego. Investing one's libido or energy in the ego can only lead to bankruptcy of the self. When Arthur ran out of energy to support his image, it began to crack. Yet he could not give it up. He was in serious trouble.

In our consultation, I described the nature of the problem to Arthur and stressed the need for ongoing therapy. Without treatment, his condition could only deteriorate. Unfortunately, I never saw him again, and he never paid me for the consultation. "I left my checkbook at the hotel," he said, promising to send me a check. Arthur, then, clung to his denial. He had consulted me in the hope that somehow I could help him regain the energy to refurbish his image. He was looking for magic, which he thought I might have as he believed he once did. Reality was too painful for him to accept. In the world of make-believe in which he lived, there was no moral obligation to pay a doctor for his time. Life is a stage, and when the curtain falls upon an act, it is finished and forgotten. The emptiness of such a life is beyond imagination.

• • •

I have emphasized the incongruence or opposition of self and image in the narcissist. Although I prefer this way of describing the split, it may be helpful now to add the notion of a true and a false, or superficial, self. The false self rests on the surface, as the self presented to the world. It stands in contrast to the true self, which resides behind the façade or image. This true self is the feeling self, but it is a self that must be hidden and denied. Since the superficial self represents submission and conformity, the inner or true self is rebellious and angry. This underlying rebellion and anger can never be fully suppressed since it is an expression of the life force in the person. But because of the denial, it cannot be expressed directly. Instead, it shows up in the narcissist's acting out. And it can become a perverse force.

The important distinction, then, is between the person who operates in terms of an image and the person who functions in terms of his or her feelings. But since feelings are a natural attribute of being human, how can one not feel? If the image is established as the dominant force in the personality, the person will suppress any feeling that contradicts it. But an image can only gain this dominant position in the absence of strong feelings. I strongly believe that the absence of feeling is the basic disturbance in the narcissistic personality, and the one that allows the image to gain ascendancy. In narcissism, as opposed to the typical neuroses of earlier times, the loss of feeling is due to a special mechanism, which I call the denial of feeling.

3

The Denial of Feeling

WHAT does it mean not to feel? Let us begin with an extreme example—a catatonic man who stands motionless in a corner for hours like a statue. He has suppressed all feeling, including pain, which is why he can stand immobile for long periods of time. It is as if his body were in rigor mortis, without impulse or internal movement. Having deadened himself, he is anesthetized to pain. Of course, this deadening is not complete but only extends to the voluntary musculature. The other organs still function normally.

All neurotics, including narcissists, use this mechanism of deadening parts of the body to suppress feelings. One can set one's jaw to block an impulse to cry. If the set is maintained indefinitely, the jaw becomes frozen in this position and crying becomes impossible. One can suppress anger by "freezing" or deadening the muscles of the upper back and shoulders through chronic tension. Yet although this mechanism is used by narcissists, there is another, more important defense typical of this disorder—denial of feeling.

The concept of denial of feeling requires some elucidation. First, it must be recognized that a feeling is the perception of some internal bodily movement or event. If there is no such happening, there is no feeling because there is nothing to perceive. If one lets one's arm hang *motionless* for five minutes, it will become numb and one will not feel one's arm. To regain feeling, one must move one's arm. Thus, by inhibiting movement, one can deaden oneself, much like the catatonic I described. But there is another way to cut off the access of impulses and actions to consciousness: One can block the function of perception. This is the mechanism by which feelings are denied.

A common example of the denial of feeling is a person who shouts and yells in a discussion as if he or she were angry. But when one asks what he or she is angry about, the person answers: "Who's angry?" The explanation I would offer is that this person's image is of a rational and logical being; nothing is allowed to enter consciousness that might contradict this image. Another example is a young psychologist I know. This man kept trying to convince me that he was a great therapist. Every time we met he harangued me with "I know," "I can do that," etc. Almost every sentence began with the word "I," in typical narcissistic fashion. Whenever I became annoyed and pointed out his narcissism, he countered with the argument that I refused to recognize his superiority. He refused to see his narcissistic need to impress me. To sense his desperate need for approval might undermine his image.

The need to project and maintain an image forces the person to prevent any feeling from reaching consciousness that would conflict with the image. Behavior that might contradict the image is rationalized in terms of the image. Thus, our angry person might explain the "necessity" of shouting by saying: "People weren't really listening. They didn't hear me. I was simply trying to present my views." Similarly, the young psychologist rationalized his behavior by blaming me. In a normal person, actions are associated with the feelings that motivated them. In the narcissistic individual, however, the action is dissociated from the feeling or impulse and justified by the image.

THE EFFECT ON BEHAVIOR TOWARD OTHERS

The denial of feeling characteristic of all narcissists is most manifest in their behavior toward others. They can be ruthless, exploitative, sadistic, or destructive to another person because they are insensitive to the other's suffering or feeling. This insensitivity derives from an insensitivity to one's own feelings. Empathy, the ability to sense other people's moods or feelings, is a function of resonance. We can feel another person's sadness because it makes us sad; we can share another's joy because it evokes good feelings in us. But if we are incapable of feeling sadness or joy, we cannot respond to these feelings in another person, and we may even doubt that they have such feelings. When we deny our feelings, we deny that others feel.

Only on this basis can we explain the ruthless behavior of some narcissists like the corporate executives who drive their employees remorselessly and create a reign of terror by their indifference to human sensibilities and indiscriminate firings, without regard for people's feelings. Of course, they are equally hard on themselves; their goals of power and success demand an equal sacrifice of their own sensibilities and feelings. These executives see themselves as generals in some war in which business success spells victory. With such an image of themselves, they can only treat their subordinates as dispensable soldiers in the drive to win.

One of the ways in which our culture fosters the narcissistic personality is by its exaggerated emphasis upon the importance of winning. There is a popular slogan that says winning is the only thing that counts. Such an attitude minimizes human values and subordinates the feelings of others to this one overriding goal to win, to be on top, to be number one. But the commitment to this goal also demands the sacrifice or denial of one's own feelings, for nothing must stand in the way of winning. However, the image of success derives its power to dominate behavior only when feelings are denied. We are confronted with that old dilemma: Which came first, the chicken or the egg? In this case, the same question can be asked: Which came first, the image or the denial of feelings? The answer to these questions is that each is an aspect of the other. Without the denial of feeling, the image would not gain its position of dominance, but only when it does become dominant are feelings continually denied.

Behavior that is injurious to or destructive of others can only be fully understood in terms of the denial of feeling, the goal of winning, and the image of power. Executives who exploit their employees and con artists who swindle elderly pensioners operate on the same principle. Both fail to see others as real people; in their eyes, others exist only as objects to be used. Specifically, the elderly pensioners are not seen as human beings, because the swindlers don't see themselves in human terms. They live by their wits and are identified with their ability to outsmart or outmaneuver others. That they lie or cheat is unimportant to the goal of winning or their ego image of superiority based on their ability to put one over on another person.

The connection between the overriding importance of winning, the denial of feeling, and the role of the image is most evident in warfare. Since victory or defeat is seen as a matter of life or death, there is no room for feelings. Soldiers function largely in terms of images. However, they retain their humanity by their feelings for a buddy or the squad members with whom they have personal contact. Without these feelings they risk becoming killing machines or going insane. A soldier is not a narcissist, but war forces him to act like one.

Unfortunately, warfare is not limited to armies fighting each other. In most large cities, there are gang wars in which the members of a gang function like soldiers denying feeling and human values. But we also have business wars, political wars, and family warfare which promote a narcissistic attitude and encourage behavior that is injurious and destructive to others. The enemy is not pictured in terms of real people, for it is not easy to kill real people. Soldiers are taught to see the enemy as an image—the "Jap," the Hun, the Nazi, etc.—which it is their duty to destroy. But to do this, they, too, must become an image. They are soldiers whose role is to obey orders, to fight but not to question, to act but not to feel. They must not let themselves feel their fear or their pain or their sadness. To be in touch with these feelings would undermine the soldier image and make it impossible for them to function effectively on the battlefield. And they cannot reject this image, for that would bring them into conflict with their leaders, which might also endanger their survival.

When one is identified with an image, one sees the other as an image that in many cases represents some rejected aspect of the self. Narcissism splits the reality of an individual into accepted and rejected aspects, the latter being projected, then, upon others. The attack upon these others stems partly from the desire to destroy this rejected aspect. For example, the con man who thinks of himself as shrewd and superior must see his victim as gullible and stupid. Similarly the soldier whose image is of fighting for the right, for justice and for honor will, often, see the enemy as cruel and dishonorable. If the narcissistic image is one of toughness and strength, one will project upon others an image of vulnerability and weakness which must be destroyed.

Does this principle also explain acts of gratuitous violence in peacetime? A case in point was the action of a gang of boys who set fire to an old vagrant sleeping on a park bench. It was such an inhuman act that most people were shocked and confounded by it. Where were their feelings? Obviously, they had none for the old man. They did not see him as a real person but only as an image, an image of decrepit age which they found repulsive and so destroyed. But unlike soldiers who have no personal contact with the human beings they kill, these boys were in the presence of a living person. In killing him so wantonly, they denied his humanity and in the process denied their own. Most likely they had lost their humanity before they committed this crime. Most probably the horror and insanity of their own lives had caused them to deny their feelings.

There is a continuous line from violence against helpless persons, to rape of helpless women, to seduction and exploitativeness. What the rapist and the seducer have in common, though to different degrees, is an insensitivity to the sexual partner, an overinvolvement with their egos and a lack of sexual feeling on a body level. Sexual feeling, as opposed to genital excitation, is experienced as love, tenderness, and the longing to be close to another person. The denial of this feeling, because of its association with neediness and vulnerability, promotes overexcitation of the genitals, leading to the act of rape. The genital charge is overpowering because the individual cannot contain the feeling. Unable to approach a woman in a state of relaxation, the rapist is driven or propelled into a violent action, which also expresses his intense hostility to women. Fearing women, the rapist is sexually aroused only by the image of aggressive power over a woman. Similarly, the seducer depends on an image for sexual arousal—the picture of an irresistible, dominant, and controlling "lover." Both types exemplify narcissistic behavior because they do not see their victims as people in their own right but only as images. Both rape and seduction are pornographic scenes in that sexual desire depends on denying the other's humanity or personhood and seeing only a sex object.

Slightly less psychopathic and violent than a rapist, but equally without feeling, was a casting director who required all young aspiring actresses to undress and engage in sexual acts with him as a condition for getting parts. The requirement of sex was not overtly stated, but the director did make some advances and the women were well aware that a failure to respond would result in rejection. The effect was rape, in that their integrity was violated and their human dignity denied. The young women were not persons to the director but only names and dames. Later, he bragged about the number of actresses, some well known, whom he had possessed. His sexual activity, however, was without feeling or pleasure. It merely gratified his image.

Moving along the line toward lesser degrees of narcissism, we find the male executive who seduces his female secretary. This is not to say that every sexual relationship between an employer and an employee is tainted with narcissism. It is a question of feeling, of love between the parties. For the male executive-seducer, sexual desire is often strong because he feels himself to be in a superior or dominant position socially. This position alleviates his fear of women and permits him to feel strongly excited on a genital level. Yet without a feeling of love or affection for his partner and respect for her feelings as a human being, the sexual act is largely a narcissistic expression. It amounts to exploitation.

Obviously, a person can be genitally excited without any real sexual feeling. The excitation is strictly limited to the genitals. A man, for example, can have an erection without any desire to be close and intimate with a woman—that is, without any feeling of love. The desire is in his head just as the excitation is in the head of his penis. Sex for such a man serves two purposes: to release the excitation in the penis (which can become painful) and to bolster a weak and inflated ego with the conquest and humiliation of a woman. Sure, it feels good to discharge sexual excitation, but the pleasure of release is strictly local, limited to the genitals. A localized feeling should more properly be called a sensation. Sexual feeling, in contrast to genital excitation, is a total body feeling of excitement, warmth, and melting at the prospect or experience of contact and intimacy with another person. When the total body responds sexually, the climax is imbued with the feeling of joy or ecstasy.

THE CONNECTION TO LYING

In the world of images, we inevitably encounter the question of fit. By itself an image has no validity. A narcissist's image of superiority has as much meaning as a conscientious person's image of integrity and honesty. An image, by definition, is a representation of something. Thus, we cannot judge an image except in terms of its relationship to the reality it purports to represent. When reality is objectifiable, this determination is easy. The circumstances of a person's birth, family, and background, for instance, are definable facts. To misrepresent them is to lie. For an impostor, however, the lie comes easily because the reality has long since been denied in an emotional sense. The impostor does not want to acknowledge an average birth and background, for that would not contradict a sense of inferiority or vulnerability. No, the impostor must be someone else, someone special and superior. It is not difficult, then, to extend this image to include the idea of nobility.

The tendency to lie, without compunction, is typical of narcissists. At an extreme is the psychopathic personality, who seems to have no sense of the difference between right and wrong on a feeling level. This is a person without a conscience or, in psychoanalytic terms, someone who lacks a superego. There is no guilt. Although most narcissists are far from this extreme, in both their subjective denial of feeling and in their use of an image that contradicts the truth of their being, they share certain similarities with psychopathic personalities. In this regard, they have lost the ability to distinguish truth from falsehood.

Let us return to our example of an impostor. This impostor holds himself out to be a nobleman, even though he knows, intellectually, that he was not born to high estate. What happens is that he sees himself as being of noble birth when he acts the part. And his acting is convincing because he has become convinced. He identifies with his image, and this becomes his only reality; he no longer senses that he is distorting or denying the truth. In effect, he denies or ignores the reality of his being, but the denial is no longer deliberate or conscious. The actor has become so identified with his role or pose that it has become real for him.

The impostor who believes he is a nobleman is a psychopath for whom subjective reality has displaced the objective reality of his birth. The narcissistic character is more in touch with objective reality but is dominated by the image. Beatrice was a case in point. As she stood before the group at a bioenergetic training workshop in Europe, she held herself up as if she were superior with a bearing that could almost be called imperious. I was not surprised, therefore, when she said that she had always thought of herself as a princess. For a moment I thought I might have had to deal with a psychopathic personality, but Beatrice then added, "I grew up in a castle." Was she, then, a real princess? Beatrice explained, "My father was an engineer who made a lot of money before I was born and bought this castle. He treated me like a princess." Beatrice was an only child.

Her problem was a lack of feeling, particularly sexual feeling. Her belly was contracted and her pelvis was held tightly, allowing little spontaneous movement. Her feelings were confined to the upper half of her body, but even here they were rigidly controlled. Beatrice related a recurrent dream in which she saw herself as a princess lying in a glass coffin. She recognized that the glass coffin was the castle and that by being made to think of herself as a princess, she was both deadened and imprisoned. Like Sleeping Beauty, she awaited a rescuer who would free her and bring her back to life. The coffin also represented the rigidity of her body in which her feelings were imprisoned. Beatrice, too, had to cry to release the sadness that was locked up in her tight belly. By getting her to breathe deeply so that the respiratory movements involved the pelvis, both her sadness and her sexuality could then be experienced and expressed.

SUPPRESSION VERSUS DENIAL OF FEELING

At the beginning of this chapter, I alluded to the difference between the suppression of feeling and the denial of feeling. One can suppress feeling by deadening the body and reducing its motility. Again, if there is no internal movement, there is nothing to feel. An emotion is a movement (motion) toward (the prefix "e" denotes an outward direction). Every emotion is movement from the center to the periphery, where it is expressed in action. The feeling of love, for example, is experienced as an impulse to reach out to someone; anger, as an impulse to strike out; sadness, to cry out. The impulse of the emotion must reach the surface of the body to be experienced as a feeling. It need not, however, produce any overt action. If the impulse sets up a state of readiness to act in the musculature, it will be experienced as an emotion. One does not have to strike out to feel angry, but the body does have to be primed for such an action. In most people, a strong feeling of anger will result in a spontaneous clenching of the fists. In others, the anger may surface as a look in the eyes. I don't believe it is possible for a person to feel an emotion and not allow some expression of it to show, however subtle it is.

Inhibiting movement through chronic muscular tension has the effect of suppressing feeling. Such tension produces a rigidity in the body, a partial deadness. It is not surprising that soldiers are drilled in standing rigidly at attention. As we have seen, a good soldier must suppress much feeling and become, in effect, a killing machine.

Because rigidity is associated with the suppression of feeling, one can tell which feelings are being suppressed by studying the pattern of tension. Tight jaw muscles, for instance, will inhibit an impulse to bite. We can guess that such persons have suppressed biting impulses as children. These impulses may, however, come through in biting sarcasm. A tight jaw will also block sucking impulses, suppressing the desire for closeness and contact. A constricted throat prevents deep sobbing and helps the person suppress sadness. Stiff shoulders diminish the intensity of an angry reaction.

Overall body rigidity deadens the body by restricting respiration and limiting the body's motility. Normally, breathing is not a conscious undertaking; the movements of expansion and contraction occur without voluntary action. Babies and young children breathe in this very natural way. But as we learn to control and suppress our feelings, we tense our bodies and inhibit this natural respiration. By doing so we reduce the intake of oxygen, diminishing metabolic activity and decreasing the energy available for spontaneous movement and feeling. We can, of course, still move by using the will, but such movement is mechanical. One finds such overall rigidity in some narcissistic individuals whose style is to pose in a statuesque manner. But many narcissistic individuals have bodies that are fairly agile and flexible. They can be actors, athletes, or jet-setters. Their bodies have a seeming aliveness and grace, suggesting the presence of emotions. Their behavior, however, is without feeling, which means that we must search for another mechanism whereby feeling is cut off. That mechanism, as I have already indicated, is to block the perceptive function rather than the movement.

Since perception is a function of consciousness, it is generally under ego control. Normally we perceive those things which interest us and ignore those which have no interest for us. We can also deliberately focus our attention on certain objects or situations to perceive them more clearly. But by the same process, we can refuse to see them or ignore them. Often the decision is made subliminally, at the margin of consciousness. For example, we rarely allow ourselves to see the pain and sadness in the faces and eyes of our loved ones. Few parents see the unhappiness in their children's faces. And children learn very quickly not to see the anger and hostility in their parents' eyes. In a similar way, as I pointed out earlier, we don't let ourselves see the expression in our own faces when we look in the mirror. We might see some wrinkles, but we close our minds to the evident despair; a man might carefully trim a mustache but not see the tight, cruel lips below it. In effect, we don't see what we don't want to see. Many people walking the streets of a large city like New York do not see the dirt or hear the noise. Their minds (attention) are focused elsewhere.

I think that one principle underlying selective perception is that we do not want to see a problem that we can do nothing about. To see the problem might put us into an intolerable state of stress or pain, which could threaten our sanity. In effect, we block out or deny some aspects of reality in self-defense. But this denial implies a previous recognition of the situation. We cannot deny that which we do not know. Denial is a secondary process. First, we see the painful situation; then, when we realize that we can neither support it nor change it, we deny its existence. We close our eyes to it.

In the beginning, then, the denial is conscious. One doesn't make a decision to deny the reality of a situation, but one is aware of its painfulness and of one's desire to avoid it. In time, however, the denial becomes unconscious; that is, one no longer senses the pain in the situation, nor sees its ugliness. Instead, one creates an image of a pleasant or happy situation, which enables one to carry on as if everything were all right. At this point, the denial becomes structured in the body as localized chronic muscular tensions rather than overall rigidity. The locus of that tension is at the base of the skull, in the muscles that bind the head to the neck. This area is close to the visual centers in the brain and has some influence on visual perception. I have often been able to help a patient visualize an angry or crazy look in a parent's eyes by applying some pressure with my fingers to these muscles. The tension in these muscles seems to block the flow of excitation from the body into the head, which is thus cut off from body feeling. The psychological effect, dissociating the ego from the body's feelings, is similar in some ways to the dissociation from reality that occurs in schizophrenia, although to a much lesser degree.

The block in perception produces a denial of feeling, which is the purpose. Evoking the feeling should remove the block, just as removing the block should lead to feeling. This is illustrated in Sally's case.

The Case of Sally

Sally, a young woman participating in a bioenergetic training workshop, described the nightmare she had lived through in the past ten years. She had been married to a man who beat her physically, ran around with other women, and threatened to take her children away if she divorced him. She was terrified of him, for he was a powerful man, physically and otherwise. But she did divorce him and keep her children. What was surprising was that in telling this story, Sally displayed very little emotion. I was also struck by the shallowness of her breathing. Although her whole body wasn't rigid, her throat was constricted. To understand the origin of this constriction, I asked her about her childhood.

Sally immediately responded that she had had a happy childhood. To date, I have never worked with anyone who had a happy childhood. I had heard such statements from a number of patients before, but they always turned out to be a denial of the reality. If Sally's childhood had been a happy one, I would not expect her to constrict her throat as if she were blocking off feeling, or to marry a man who abused her. As I have pointed out in another book,[1] most men marry women who are like their mothers, and women tend to marry men who are like their fathers. I asked Sally to tell me something about her father.

Sally used the same words to describe her father that she had used to describe her husband. He was, she said, a rather powerful man. She remembered being close to him as a child. But he drank and their relationship suffered. He became unpredictable. Because drinking men may also be violent, I asked Sally if her father ever hit her. Despite my suspicion that this might have been the case, I was somewhat startled by her answer: "He used to punch me with his fist, sometimes hitting me in the face. I never knew when a blow would come." I could see that Sally had been as terrified of her father as she later was of her husband. But since she was a child and could not leave her home, she suppressed and denied her terror. This denial of fear blinded her to the potential violence in the man she married.

The particular subject of this workshop session was breathing. I was demonstrating the connection between voice and breathing. Suppressing the expression of sound reduces one's breathing by closing the throat. Limiting one's breathing in turn decreases one's vocal production. The particular exercise I was working with involved lying over the bioenergetic stool.[2] The person is instructed, first, to breathe easily and deeply. After a number of breaths, he or she is asked to make a sound and to sustain it as long as possible. In the beginning, the sound is usually well controlled and has no emotional quality. But as the sound is prolonged, it reaches a breaking point, where it may easily turn into crying. In Sally's case, she broke into violent sobbing mixed with screams. This continued for several minutes, even after she left the stool. Such a pronounced reaction does not occur routinely; Sally was ready to release these feelings. It was the ninth day of the workshop, and considerable feeling had already been expressed by other participants.

After this breakthrough of feeling, I talked to Sally about the horror of her childhood, and she was able to *see* it for the first time. She could no longer pretend that it had been a happy period. Now she admitted the latent violence in her home and the fear it engendered. How could she be sure when the violence would erupt (which it did from time to time)? And how could her father, who proclaimed his love for her, abuse her? Believing in his love, she could not understand the split in his personality. It was incomprehensible, as insanity usually is. Sally had had to deny the horror to guard her own sanity. After this session she looked truly alive.

I do not want to give the impression, however, that this experience constituted a cure. It was a meaningful experience for Sally, enabling her to see both the depth of her problem and a way out. That way out would take considerable work, often extending over several years, in the course of which Sally would deepen her insight, sense the feelings she had denied, and learn to express them without becoming overwhelmed. Therapy is a process of extending self-awareness, increasing self-expression, and achieving self-possession, which is the ability to contain and sustain strong feelings. Bodily tensions and rigidity have to be gradually reduced so that the body can tolerate the higher level of excitation associated with strong feelings. I believe the best approach to this objective is one that combines analysis with intensive body work.

DEGREES OF FEELING

Perhaps you are wondering: Can any human being act totally without feeling? Does the denial of feeling mean the denial of *all* feeling? Only a machine can operate without any feeling or consciousness whatsoever. Although some people function like machines, with cool efficiency and seemingly without feeling, we must recognize that feeling is potentially present. And it does manifest itself on occasion, but in distorted form. In narcissistic individuals, expressions of feeling usually take two forms: an irrational rage and a maudlin sentimentality. The rage is a distorted outbreak of anger; the sentimentality is a substitute for love. Hitler might be described as a person without feeling, but he was known for his intemperate rages. I would call his love for the German people pure sentimentality. To act without feeling is to be a monster; but true monsters, like Frankenstein's, exist only in our imagination. Human monsters are characterized by their irrational rage, their sentimentality, and their insensitivity to others. Parents who beat or torture their children are such human monsters, as we just saw in Sally's case. To guard her sanity, Sally had to deny the horror of the situation and close her eyes to the monstrous aspect of her father. She, too, had to cut off feeling, although she did this to a lesser degree.

Parents who beat their children were probably beaten as children themselves. Having denied their own feelings about that experience, they cannot experience any feeling for the child. Still, it is beyond my comprehension how parents can justify the beating of a child. I see it as an expression of cruelty. I am always horrified when I hear patients relate how they were required to fetch the switch with which the beating was administered. In the same way, I cannot understand cruelty to animals. They are sentient beings, capable of experiencing pleasure and pain, sadness and joy, fear and anger. Human beings who lack these feelings are in some way lower than animals.

Of course, on the level of feeling we do differ from animals. Our emotional life is more intense. We are capable of a greater love and a fuller hate, a higher joyfulness and a deeper sadness, a stronger fear and a more intense anger. And human beings can also "control" their feelings through their egos. We can limit the degree of feeling, and we can act as if we had feeling. But there is a problem in doing this. Emotions are total bodily responses. For that reason, one cannot suppress or deny fear, for instance, without at the same time suppressing the feeling of anger. This is an important concept for therapists to understand.

Often one sees patients who seem able to express anger but not fear or sadness. I have found that this seeming display of anger is without feeling. It is a defensive maneuver intended to frighten the other person rather than an expression of genuine emotion. In addition, by acting angry, the person denies his or her own fear. One may believe one is angry, just as impostors believe their lies or actors identify with their roles, but a genuine feeling of anger stems from a feeling of having been hurt. If one denies the hurt, what is there to be angry about? If one cannot feel one's sadness, why is one angry? My initial approach with all narcissistic patients is to help them get in touch with their sadness. This is not always an easy undertaking.

The Case of Linda

Linda, a woman close to forty, consulted me because she had been severely depressed some years ago and was afraid this was going to happen again. When she entered my office, I was impressed by her appearance. She was an attractive woman, strikingly but tastefully dressed, with a shapely figure. She smiled easily and seemed free in her manner. Granted, her voice was slightly husky, without much range of tone. Still, it was hard to believe, at first glance, that Linda had any serious problems.

Her major complaint was that she didn't seem to be getting anywhere in life. She had held the same job for a number of years. Although it was a creative position and paid her well, she felt unfulfilled. She thought she should move on, get a job with more responsibility and more money. But she didn't know what else she wanted to do. She was also dissatisfied with her personal life. She had never married and felt desperate about the prospect of never having a family. Yet she wasn't sure if that was her most important goal. She was confused about her direction in life, caught between her desire for a career and her wish for a home. Some women, she commented, achieve both, but she hadn't attained either. On the surface, Linda seemed to have the potential for both—brains and beauty. What was wrong?

Linda's present depressive reaction had begun just after the breakup of a relationship with a man. She hadn't been in love with him; she herself had terminated the relationship because it wasn't going anywhere. Nevertheless, she experienced the breakup as a failure and became depressed.

The first cue I had to Linda's problem was her voice. I had noticed its lack of resonance. I could not sense any excitement in her voice; it sounded unalive. When I remarked on this to Linda in our first session, she replied, "I've always been ashamed of my voice. It doesn't sound right." The voice, as I have indicated, is one of the main channels of self-expression. The lack of resonance in her voice suggested a lack of feeling in her body.

Since Linda had said that she was unhappy and frustrated about her life situation, I suggested that she try to express some feeling about this. Could she voice some protest about her fate? I asked her to lie on the bed* and kick her legs against it as a form of protest. To kick about something means to protest. This is one of the regular exercises in bioenergetic therapy. All patients have something to kick about. Neurotic individuals suppress their feelings, and kicking is one way to help them express these feelings. The voice is also engaged in this exercise. With the kicking, the person is told to say "No" or "Why?" Both words imply a protest. I specifically directed Linda to raise her voice as loud as possible, letting it come out as a yell or scream.

Linda tried the exercise, but her kicking was mechanical and her voice sounded weak. It lacked any note of conviction. She complained that she had no feeling of protest in her, so she couldn't do the exercise properly. Did she have any feeling of sadness which she could express by crying? She didn't feel sad and she couldn't cry. Nor could she feel any anger. In fact, she didn't feel any emotion strongly enough to be able to express it. That was her problem.

I realized that Linda's appearance was a façade. She projected the image of a successful woman of the world, but the image did not correspond to her inner being. I could guess that in her inner being she felt herself to be a failure. The fear of failure had led to her first depressive reaction. For some reason, the image was so important to her that it absorbed most of her energy, leaving her without the strength to express herself with feeling as a real person in the world.

* In bioenergetic analysis, a bed is used instead of a couch because the expressive exercises such as hitting or kicking the bed cannot be done on a couch.

To help Linda, I had to understand both the exact meaning of the image and its relation to her sense of self. What was the image of success so effectively concealing? Why and how did it assume such an overriding importance in Linda's life? What did failure signify? It is insufficient to answer these questions in general terms. The narcissistic image develops in part as a compensation for an unacceptable self-image and in part as a defense against intolerable feelings. These two functions of the image are fused, for the unacceptable self-image is associated with the intolerable feelings. It was only as Linda's therapy progressed that we came to understand the exact meaning and role of her success image.

Therapy is a process of getting in touch with the self. Traditionally, the approach to the self has been through analysis. Every therapy must include a thorough analysis of the patient's history to discover the experiences that have shaped the patient's personality and determined his or her behavior. Unfortunately, that history is not readily available. The suppression and denial of feeling result in a repression of significant memories. The façades we erect hide our true selves from us as well as from the world. But analysis has other material to work with, in addition to remembered history.

The analysis of dreams is one way to acquire additional data. Then there is the analysis of present-day behavior, especially as it is evidenced in the therapeutic relationship. This relationship is often a highly emotional one because feelings toward important figures from the past, like the parents, are transferred to the analyst. Through analysis patients come to see the connections between their adult attitudes and actions and their childhood experiences. This traditional approach, however, is limited because it is too dependent on words, which are themselves only symbols or images.

Getting in touch with the self involves more than analysis. The self is not a mental construct but a bodily phenomenon. To be in touch with oneself means to sense and be in touch with one's feelings. To know one's feelings, one has to experience them in their full intensity and that can only be done by expressing them. If the expression of a feeling is blocked or inhibited, the feeling is either suppressed or diminished. It is one thing to talk about fear, another to *feel* the fright and scream. Saying "I am angry" is *not* the same thing as feeling the emotion surge through one's body. To truly feel one's sadness, one has to cry. This is what Linda was unable to do. She had choked off her sobs and her screams. She had swallowed her tears. The chronic tension in her throat affected her speaking voice, making it sound unalive.

In addition to verbal analysis, then, Linda's therapy involved working with her body physically to reduce its rigidity, to deepen her breathing, and to open her throat.

I have mentioned earlier in this chapter some of the exercises I use—kicking the bed while saying "no" as an expression of protest and hitting the bed to express anger. These are expressive exercises. They would also include reaching out with one's hands to touch, to call for mother or to ask for help, and reaching out with the lips to kiss or suck. Most people have a lot of trouble reaching out; they are inhibited by a fear of rejection which is structured in tensions around the shoulders and the mouth. I also use a number of positions to help a person feel his body from head to toe. The simplest of these is a standing position with the feet parallel and about six inches apart, the knees slightly bent, the weight of the body on the balls of the feet, the belly out and the pelvis slightly back. If the person will breathe easily and deeply with the shoulders relaxed, he will feel himself down to his feet. It is the position to which one lets oneself down from the rigid holding of oneself up. Many people doing this exercise feel some anxiety about letting go or letting down. One can then sense how tightly one holds to maintain control. Another position, called grounding, enables a person to feel his contact with the floor or earth. The person bends forward and touches the floor with the points of the fingers. The feet are parallel and about twelve inches apart, the knees slightly bent. Again, breathing deeply and freely is important. If one feels one's legs in an alive way in this exercise, they will vibrate as the current of excitation flows through them. The vibration reduces the tension in the legs and gives the person a sense of aliveness in the lower part of the body. All exercises must be attuned to the needs of the person as they are manifested in the expression of the body. Such work with the body aims at and facilitates the release of feeling. And this release often brings to consciousness a significant memory from the past. The release of feeling removes the block in the function of perception.

After a number of sessions and considerable work, Linda broke through her throat block. As she noted, "I was able to cry with deep sobbing, and I experienced a lot of sadness. I recalled that as a child I was so frightened because Mom and Dad argued so much. I was terrified that either he would hurt her or she him. I always tensed up in bed when they were arguing, petrified or terrified that one of them would get hurt, possibly killed. But I couldn't express my feelings, my fear, or my pain. Did I subconsciously want Daddy to kill Mother so I could have him all to myself?"

In the following session we looked at this problem more closely. Linda commented on the two areas where she felt stuck—her love life and her career. At the time she was living with a man who was still attached to his ex-wife, who drank and didn't have a place of his own—not even a mailing address. She remarked, "I feel stifled that he is still with me all the time. I think I love him, or at least I need him." With respect to her work, she said, "I'm having a problem with my career—I need a change. I don't want to be doing the same thing next year or five years from now, and that frightens me. I am really desperate. I'm not feeling suicidal, but I have bouts of despondency." When I asked her if she felt like a failure, she replied, "Of course I do." I then asked if she was able to cry about it, and she began to sob softly. She said it made her sad to realize she had shut off her feelings.

As we turned to the relationship with her father, the question of sex came up. Linda recalled, "When I was a child, I felt that masturbation was evil. I felt sneaky sitting on someone's knee—possibly an uncle's—and feeling good. But I have no memory of my father's physical affection—he never held me.

"My parents would accuse each other of being wrong," she continued, "and I as a child had to listen to each side separately. They would complain about the other to me, a little ten-year-old child, and tell *me* how they felt. Naturally I suppressed ever expressing how I felt. I never had the courage to tell them to shut up when they were arguing. It was an intolerable situation. I feel he was the instigator since it was his gambling that brought on the arguments—and at the same time, I could not tolerate her when she argued. I used to go to bed at night with a pillow over my head to shut off their screaming. I even remember that when I was about six or eight, I wanted to commit suicide because I couldn't stand the arguing. I was afraid he would hit her. But they never really hit each other."

Linda's story, however, did not seem complete. She reacted to the conflict between her parents as if it had a nightmarish quality. She described it as "intolerable," saying she was petrified and had wished to "die." Yet parental arguing is too commonplace in and of itself to be a horror story. Why, then, do many patients report their experience of parental fighting as a horror? The child fears that such arguing will result in one of the parents being killed. Linda indicated this fear, which I then related to the Oedipal situation. She had suspected the connection. In the Oedipal period, at three to six years of age, children have death wishes against the parent of the same sex.[3] At the same time, the child feels terribly guilty about these feelings and tries to reject them. I thus assumed that Linda had been afraid her father would kill her mother because on some level she wished he would so that she could have him all to herself. On a conscious level, however, Linda turned against her father and wished he would die. She even said that she still wished this, for it would make her mother's life much easier. But in turning against her father, Linda also turned against herself, against her love for him and against her sexuality, which was an expression of that love. At least, this was my hypothesis. To test it, I checked her feelings toward me, for as her therapist, I was a father surrogate.

As Linda lay on the bed, I leaned over her, with my face about twelve inches from hers. As our eyes made contact, I could sense that she looked at me with a positive regard. I asked her if she would like to kiss me. (I don't kiss my patients, but I do permit them to express their feelings verbally.) Linda said she was afraid to kiss me, that it was improper and "dirty." But as she said this, she began to cry and sob. She was in a conflict about her feelings. If she could not accept them, she could at least protest. So I suggested that she kick the bed and scream "Why?" After this exercise, which she did with some feeling, Linda felt some release.

In the next session, I asked Linda to reach up and touch my face. Here are her words about the experience as she recorded it in her notes after the session: "Big breakthrough came when I had to hold his face and tell him I like him. I couldn't do it. The words were choked in my throat—they wouldn't come up—and when I finally got them out, I cried. I really cried hard before I was able to say anything. I could not say 'I love you.' I could not bring the words up past my throat. But as I sobbed, I said, 'What am I afraid of? Why can't I say I love you?' I can really feel my sadness."

I told Linda that I sensed she didn't feel she had a right to burden anyone with her sadness. Her attitude in the face of sorrow was to put on a "happy face," to keep smiling. She then remarked, "My parents told me all their problems and how upset they were. I naturally felt I shouldn't share any of my upsets with them. Consequently, I pushed all my sad feelings down. Why couldn't I tell my parents I was unhappy and sad that they argued all the time and felt miserable? I can see now why I have such a neurosis about my voice and throat—including a great fear that I could develop throat cancer. I never felt like an articulate person."

After this session, in her notes Linda wrote, "I was finally able to break down. It was sad and painful, but I felt uplifted and wonderful when I left—and remained so the rest of the day."

We can see now that Linda's image and her inner reality were opposites. The image presented to the world was one of a worthy, competent, and successful person. She was a "somebody." Unfortunately, Linda didn't feel worthwhile; she didn't feel she had the right to express herself as a person, to have a voice in her own affairs. Had she felt this, there would not have been a problem. But at the beginning of her therapy, I couldn't tell what she felt. She had suppressed all feeling. Only after the experiences I have described was she able to open up and reveal her inner self.

The true sense of self is determined by the feelings of the body. And it is reflected in the body's expression. I mentioned that Linda was an attractive woman. In one respect, however, her body was misshapen. Her pelvis and buttocks were too heavy and too large. There was a passive quality about this area, and in fact, it was difficult for her to move her pelvis easily and freely. Linda was aware of this difficulty, having experienced the passivity of the lower part of her body during sexual encounters. (She had never reached a climax with a man during sexual intercourse.) The passivity related to a feeling that sexually she was "there" for the man but not for herself. When we discussed the significance of her pelvic immobility, Linda remarked that her mother had the same problem. Was she, then, identified with her mother? "I suppose we're alike in some way," Linda replied, "but I've always tried to be different from her." The difference was expressed in the role that Linda adopted, in the image she projected. The similarities, however, came out on the bodily level and in patterns of behavior that were unconsciously determined. Both women were sexually passive, suggesting deep feelings of sexual guilt, which foster feelings of inferiority and inadequacy. Belonging to the modern generation, Linda rebelled against her "fate," in contrast to her mother, who accepted hers, married, and raised a family. But Linda had to pay a price for her rebellion—namely, no marriage and no children.

I posed a question earlier about Linda's image: What was its exact meaning? To be a successful woman meant to be different from her mother. Failure meant that she was no better than her mother. But how does the idea of competition between mother and daughter (or father and son) arise? I do not believe that it is natural.* In the natural order, children tend to emulate their parents, not compare themselves with them. Competing with or comparing oneself with a parent implies an equality of level. Children can only feel equal to their parents if they are treated as equals by one or both parents. Both parents did this to Linda, sharing their problems and anxieties with her. The parent who looks for under-

* I believe the Oedipal situation is more or less universal in our culture but that does not make it natural. As I pointed out in my previous book *Fear of Life*, it derives from the power struggles in the family. It is natural for every child to have sexual feelings for the parent of the opposite sex, but these feelings do not, in my opinion, lead to a competitive situation with the parent of the same sex. That situation results from the parent's jealousy at the attention showed the child by the other parent who is seductive with the child. Once seduction occurs, the child is placed in a competitive position with the parent of the same sex.

standing and sympathy from a child treats the child as an equal, placing the child in an adult position. A similar situation occurs when a parent shows that he or she is sexually excited by a child. In both cases, the child is seduced and used. The effect, however, is to make the child feel special. That is what happened with Linda.

Linda's therapy continued to progress in a satisfactory manner. She was able to sense and express more feeling. She cried more easily and more deeply about her past and present life. Through the body work with her pelvis, she developed more sexual feeling. Then, she met a successful man, unlike her previous lovers, who was interested in marrying her. Her marriage necessitated a move to another city, and her therapy with me ended.

Linda's case illustrates a number of points about narcissism. The grandiose self-image that characterizes the narcissist compensates for an inadequate and ineffective sense of self. It represents a conscious effort to be different (better), but it fails to change the basic personality or the self. The self is a function of the body's aliveness; it is not subject to conscious control. All one can do consciously is to alter one's appearance—in effect, change one's image—and this has only a superficial effect on the personality, just as changing one's clothes does not change one's body underneath. More profound change requires the expression of the suppressed and denied feelings. To do this, one must release the chronic muscular tensions that block feeling and raise the repressed memories to consciousness.

This procedure is the basic therapeutic approach to all neurotic problems, including narcissism. But no therapeutic procedure is effective if the therapist does not understand the patient as a person. Every character problem develops through the interaction or interweaving of many forces, each of which stems from some important early life experience. Each thread of the personality fabric must be sorted out, its origin determined and its function elucidated. In Linda's case, the role of the image as a compensation for a sense of inadequacy was clarified. As Linda worked through the origins of her fears and guilts, mainly sexual, she was able to function with more feeling and with less concern for her image. Her narcissism decreased. She felt less of a need to deny her feelings.

The image itself is a denial of one's feelings. By identifying with a grandiose image, one can ignore the painfulness of one's inner reality. But the image also serves an external function in relation to the world. It is a way of gaining acceptance from others, a way of seducing them and of gaining power over them.

4

Power and Control

A STRIVING for power and control characterizes all narcissistic individuals. Not every narcissist gains power and not every person with power is a narcissist, but a need for power is part of the narcissistic disorder. What is the relation between narcissism and power?

In the preceding chapter, we saw that narcissism develops from the denial of feeling. Although the denial of feeling affects all feeling, two emotions in particular are subject to severe inhibition—sadness and fear. They are singled out because their expression makes the person feel vulnerable. To express sadness leads to an awareness of loss and evokes longing. To long for someone or to need someone leaves the person open to possible rejection and humiliation. Not wanting or not feeling desire is a defense against possible hurt. The denial of fear has a similar objective. If one doesn't feel afraid, one doesn't feel vulnerable; presumably, one can't be hurt. The denial of sadness and fear enables the person to project an image of independence, courage, and strength. This image hides the person's vulnerability from him- or herself and from others. The image, however, is only a façade and therefore impotent. In itself an image has no force—that resides in the strength of the individual's feelings.

Lacking the effective force of strong feelings, the narcissist needs and seeks power to make up the deficiency. Power seems to energize the narcissist's image, to give it a potency it would not otherwise have. One of my classmates at medical school was a small man, about five feet two inches in height. To compensate for his physical smallness, he developed a grandiose image of himself. While still a first-year student, he declared his intention to resolve the mystery of consciousness. His grandiosity also showed itself in an interesting detail. Where most of us use the expression "It's six of one, a half dozen of another" to express equality, this man always said, "It's twelve of one, a dozen of another." True, this remark in itself hardly impressed people with his bigness, but it revealed his preoccupation with large size. More clearly designed to impress was the fact that at a time and in a place where few people had cars and those who did had small ones, this man drove a big Buick. Through the power of his car, he felt and projected an image of bigness. With enough money or power, one can endow any image with seeming significance and force. With a bomb or a gun, the weakest people can see themselves as a powerful force in the world. And in fact they are. They have a power to destroy that the average person doesn't have.

All of us are vulnerable to being hurt, rejected, or humiliated. Yet not all of us deny our feelings, try to project an image of invulnerability and superiority, or strive for power. The difference lies in our childhood experiences. As children, narcissists suffer what analysts describe as a severe narcissistic injury, a blow to self-esteem that scars and shapes their personalities. This injury entails humiliation, specifically the experience of being powerless while another person enjoys the exercise of power and control over one. I don't believe that a single experience shapes character, but when a child is constantly exposed to humiliation in one form or another, the fear of humiliation becomes structured in the body and in the mind. Such a person could easily vow: "When I grow up, I'll get power, and neither you nor anyone else will be able to do this to me again." Unfortunately, as we shall see, such narcissistic injuries happen to many children in our society because parents often use power to control their children for their own personal ends.

For narcissists, control serves the same function as power —it protects them from possible humiliation. First, they control themselves by denying those feelings which might make them vulnerable. But they also have to control situations in which they find themselves; they have to make sure that there is no possibility that some other person will have power over them. Power and control are two sides of the same coin. Together, they work to protect the individual from feeling vulnerable, from feeling powerless to prevent a possible humiliation.

The Case of Clara

In a recent consultation, Clara, a borderline personality, described an experience with her therapist in which she became frightened when he put his hand on the back of her neck to release the tension in that area. She explained her fright by saying that a lot of things were done to her behind her back. When I asked her what kind of things, she replied, "My parents were contemplating putting me in a mental hospital without telling me. This was when I was seventeen. On another occasion, when I was fourteen and away at camp, they changed my high school without asking me."

I learned that the idea of the hospitalization had actually been proposed by Clara's therapist at the time. Clara explained that she had started seeing a therapist because she was disturbed: "I was extremely angry and rebellious at the time. My parents had divorced a year earlier, and my father had remarried. The divorce proceedings were ugly. My mother was barred from her home and branded an adulteress. I was living with my father at the time. When my stepmother made an insulting remark about my mother's adultery, I hit her."

Hospitalization had been suggested because Clara had become somewhat disoriented and seemed unable to coordinate her movements. It was discovered, however, that her condition was drug-induced, a side effect of a medication that had been prescribed for her. Hospitalization thus became unnecessary.

When Clara related these incidents involving things done to her behind her back, I asked her how she felt about it. "Do you feel angry?" "No," she said, "I feel powerless."

Clara then admitted that she had felt powerless all her life—not helpless but powerless. She recalled a workshop she had attended two years earlier. The participants were given a ten-minute exercise, which involved telling their fathers off. Each person was to express all his or her negative feelings about father in a loud voice. Clara described how she opened her mouth, but no sound came out. She couldn't do it. She had no voice. As a child, she had never had a voice in her own affairs, and to some extent she still didn't. Even now, she couldn't yell or shout.

Although Clara could not deliberately mobilize her protest or her anger, she could react in narcissistic, rebellious rage and strike her stepmother. Hers was a hysterical reaction (different from hysteria) because she was out of control. I shall discuss this reaction more fully later in this chapter. At this point, we should recognize Clara's behavior as a reaction to her sense of powerlessness.

How does one come to feel so powerless? Who was Clara's father? What sort of person was he? According to Clara, "He was a bull. He's a person who controls people. He always appears as a nice guy, and most people see him that way, but he causes so much disorder. In business he is ruthless. His only trip is power—power and money. He is rather handsome but big and burly. When he was angry, he was very frightening."

From Clara's description, I would venture that her father was a narcissist, a rather rich and successful one. Clara's family lived in a small community of other rich and successful people. In depicting this environment, Clara commented, "When I was eighteen and a half, I ran away from home and experimented with drugs, LSD, et cetera. I hung out with the wrong people. But so many kids my age from my hometown are crazy. One is a drug addict and dealer, another is a dishwasher. These are all from rich homes."

Clara, then, had taken a different route from her father. One difference between the narcissistic character and the borderline personality is that the former is able to compensate for the narcissistic injury by gaining power in the world, whereas the latter, despite efforts to achieve a position of power, remains with a deep feeling of powerlessness. Of course this distinction is one of degree—the narcissist is not all-powerful and the borderline personality is not completely powerless.

CHILDHOOD HUMILIATION AND FAMILY POWER STRUGGLES

Clara's account suggests that as a child she felt humiliated. All my narcissistic patients have had the experience of being deeply humiliated in childhood by parents who used power as a means of control. In many cases, the power is physical force; the parents use their superior physical strength to force the child into submission. Spankings are a common form of such physical abuse and can be particularly humiliating if the child is forced to expose his or her backside to the blows. Not infrequently the child is spanked with a hairbrush or a strap, which I regard as unnecessarily cruel treatment. Sometimes the humiliation is increased by making the child fetch the instrument of punishment or by threatening to increase the punishment if the child tries to escape. There are parents who intensify the beating if the child cries, as if to deny the child even the right to express hurt. I have been shocked by some of the stories I've heard from my patients. In most cases, the punishment so far exceeded the nature of the offense that I could not but see it as a demonstration of power: "I will teach you not to oppose me in the future." Occasionally I have detected a sadistic element in the punishment, when the patient's story indicated that the parent actually enjoyed inflicting the pain upon the child.

Of course physical punishment is not the only way to humiliate a child. Frequently children are criticized in a manner that makes them feel worthless, inadequate, or stupid. Such criticism serves no useful purpose; it is intended, in my opinion, to prove the parent's superiority. Some parents will laugh at or mock a child when the child makes a mistake or fails to give an answer that the parent thinks the child should know. When the child cries, the parent may dismiss the child's feelings as spurious, making some sarcastic comment about "crocodile tears." The list of ways children can be put down, beaten, broken, and denied respect for their humanity and selfhood is long. And many parents think there is nothing wrong in this attitude. It passes as the right thing in bringing up a child. Of course, when it comes down to physical abuse that sends a child to the hospital, we are all shocked.

The question inevitably arises: Why do parents behave in this fashion? Children learn more effectively with understanding and kindness than with force and punishment. And if punishment is necessary, it can be done in such a way as not to humiliate a child. One of the answers I would offer is that parents act out on their children the kind of treatment they received from their parents. It must also be recognized that children are the easiest and most available objects upon which parents can vent their frustrations and resentments. Parents who feel powerless in the world can compensate for this feeling by being dictatorial with their children. But however valid these answers are, I don't believe they tell the whole story. What has made for the increase in narcissistic disturbances, compared with former times?

I believe the resort to power in the upbringing of children, while not new, has taken on a different note in recent years. The reason is the increasing breakdown of authority in the home and in the community, a process that began at the end of World War I. By authority I mean respected authority. When a parent's authority is respected because that is the established practice in the community, the issue of power is less likely to arise. The parents speak not only in a personal sense but also with the voice of the community. Then power is derived from the community and exercised on behalf of the community. Because they are accountable for their behavior toward their children, they cannot so easily misuse their power.

The breakdown of authority is widespread in Western culture; it is not just limited to the home. The result has been an increasing recourse to power. Where power is the ultimate authority, whether in a nation or at home, the regime is authoritarian. But hasn't the use of force or power always been the final arbiter? That is true when the issue becomes focused on power. Yet democratic regimes have demonstrated that conflicts can be resolved without recourse to power. And throughout generations, families have followed codes of behavior that were not based on parental power so much as social cohesion.

An emphasis on parental power inevitably leads to rebellion or submission on the part of children. The submission covers an inner rebelliousness and hostility. The child who submits learns that relationships are governed by power, which sets the stage for a striving for power as an adult. Children quickly learn to play the same game as their parents—the power game. The best way to gain power over a parent is to do something that upsets the parent like not eating, not doing well at school, or smoking. Faced with such "quietly" destructive behavior, parents often become desperate and offer to give the child what he or she wants if the child yields. But since yielding means a loss of power, the threat of rebellion must be always present. Once a power struggle develops between a parent and a child, neither can yield and neither can win.

The conflict between parent and child generally stems from the parent's desire to shape the child in accord with some image in the parent's mind and the child's resistance to this effort. The use of superior force by the parent is only one of the tactics employed in this struggle. At a very young age, children are helpless and completely dependent; they can easily be controlled through any strong expression of parental disapproval, or by physical force and punishment. With older children, seduction may be increasingly employed as a means to keep control. A promise of specialness and intimacy is offered if the child will go along with the parent's wishes.

That was the pattern in my childhood. When I was very young, my mother pinched me to keep me still and make me yield to her wishes. Then as a young boy, I was punished for disobedience by being made to stay indoors when I wanted to go out and play with other children. Later, however, my mother let me know how important I was to her. Instead of asserting power through force, she shared her pain and disappointments with me. She expressed her hope that I would take care of her when she got older. I was to fulfill her dreams as my father had not. I knew I was special to her. And in some ways I fulfilled those dreams.

The struggle for power between a parent and child is usually part of the bigger struggle for power that goes on between husband and wife. The war of the sexes takes place mostly in the family. Such a struggle went on between my mother and my father. My father wanted sex and pleasure from my mother. But she wanted him to bring home more money. Her power lay in withholding sex. She made him ask for it and yielded grudgingly. But my father retaliated. His power lay in his control of the money. He made my mother ask for it, and he doled it out grudgingly. She humiliated him on one level, and he humiliated her on another. It was a cat-and-dog fight, which went on until I grew up and left home, after which, it seems, they resigned themselves to the situation.

Each parent appealed to me to understand his or her position. And I did understand. My mother was justified in her demand that she be given a definite allowance each week to run the household. My father was justified in claiming that he worked like a "dog" to make what little he did, and that he deserved some pleasure. He did work hard, although inefficiently. I was torn by their struggle, just as Linda was torn by the struggle in her family. The effect on me was twofold. I realized that money represented power, and I became determined to make enough money so that I could not be humiliated by a woman. However, out of sympathy for my mother's position, I could not easily use money as a means of control.

But why should I fear humiliation by a woman? Why should I have to prove my worth to be entitled to her sexual favors? The answer is that I felt guilty about my sexual desires. I was made to feel ashamed of my sexual feelings, and I was indoctrinated with my mother's antisexual bias. She believed that a man used a woman sexually. But why did I buy her bias, since sexual feelings were a source of pleasure for me? Two reasons suggest themselves. One is an unfulfilled oral longing which made me want to be close to her at almost any cost. The second is her offer of specialness which I could not resist. The effect was to make me insecure about my sexuality and, thus, to undermine my manhood.

Now I was special and superior on one hand, but insecure and ashamed on the other. If I presented myself in the superior pose, I was afraid that I could be exposed as the opposite. Every narcissist has his deep fear of humiliation because his grandiose image covers an underlying sense of inadequacy.

Power is a way to protect oneself against humiliation. It is a means of overcoming a feeling of inferiority. It is an antidote for sexual impotence. This last statement should not be read to mean that every person who has power is sexually impotent. It does mean that individuals who are sexually impotent wish or openly strive for power.

The child who is made to feel special becomes the center of the parental power struggle, and his position becomes particularly critical during the Oedipal period.* If he is a boy, he becomes a competitor of his father since he is set up as superior to his father by his mother. A girl becomes the rival of her mother for her father's love through his special interest in her. As a result, the child is trapped in a desperate situation. There is always the danger of the same-sex parent's hostility on one side and on the other a fear of incest or humiliating rejection if one responded sexually to the seduction. In almost all cases, the seductive parent is also a rejecting parent. At this age, the fear of incest is the physical fear of the seemingly powerful adult genital organ. Unfortunately, there is no way out of this kind of Oedipal situation for a child except by cutting off sexual feelings. The child doesn't cut off genitality but sexuality—that is, the melting sensations in the pelvis, which are the basis of sexual love. But this cutting off of feeling amounts to a psychological

* In my book *Fear of Life*, I showed how the acquisition of power by human beings created the Oedipal situation, which stems from the struggle for power in the family. Through power, man asserted his domination over nature and over women, whom he identified with nature. Politically, women became second-class citizens, and under Roman law their property belonged to their husbands. Women today are still struggling against the injustices of this system.

castration and leaves the person orgastically impotent. I strongly believe that this impotence is the basis, on the deepest level, of the striving for power.

To be subject to another person's power is a humiliating experience. This insult to the person's ego can be wiped out only by reversing the situation—namely, by gaining power over the person who inflicted the narcissistic injury. A person can, of course, submit to the domination, but such submission covers a deep hate. Obviously, there can be no love in a relationship when power plays an important role.

These considerations are important to an understanding of the power struggles that go on in families. In these fights, the issue is rarely the right or wrong of an action but who is going to have his or her way. In the early years of a child's life, the parent is stronger and will usually win. But the parent's victory doesn't end the struggle in most cases. As the child grows older and stronger, he or she will challenge the parent again and again in an effort to destroy the parent's power and to gain power over the parent. These fights are extremely destructive to family relationships and to the individuals involved. Yet as long as power is an issue in the family, they are inevitable.

A typical scenario might be:

CHILD: Can I watch TV?
MOTHER: No.
CHILD: Why?
MOTHER: You have to do your homework.
CHILD: But I don't have any homework today. So can I watch TV now?
MOTHER: No.
CHILD: Why?
MOTHER: Because I said no! That's enough reason.

This statement is the final word. The mother wants to be obeyed and not have her decisions constantly challenged, as children will do. It is important for her to show firmness and authority, in the sense of "no questions asked." She believes that to vacillate would betray weakness and give the child power over her. She would lose control of the child, who would then become a wild, destructive creature, impossible to control. Control must be maintained at all times, and the only way to do that is to assert one's power. Mother must always know best. She is not to be contradicted. Dictatorial regimes use a similar line of reasoning to justify their use of power to control people.

THE OVEREMPHASIS ON POWER IN SOCIETY

We have looked at how the narcissist's striving for power stems from a deep sense of humiliation suffered as a child. But to say this doesn't help us to understand the origin of power struggles per se. Even when parents start with the best of intentions, power struggles seem to develop. Are they inevitable? My thesis is that such struggles are inherent in an emphasis on the acquisition of power for its own sake.

Just as contemporary Western culture promotes narcissism, it is a culture geared to and obsessed with power. Today's civilization and mode of life would be impossible without the tremendous energy and power (fuel and machines) available to do work. In the past, the possession of power was clearly restricted to relatively few persons: kings, nobles, merchants, bishops, etc. They had their horses, their slaves, and their servants, but quantitatively speaking, their power was small compared with what can be commanded today. For example, an average American commands more horsepower in his or her automobile than any Victorian squire did with his stables and servants. Of course, relatively speaking, the squire had a greater sense of power than an automobile owner does. However, we should not minimize the sense of power that stems from the possession and control of a machine. The thrill of a high-powered motorcycle lies in the sense of power it provides its owner. What English noble could traverse the Atlantic as easily as one can do today? Technology has provided modern man with a sense of power that he never had before. The question is: How does such accessible power affect the psychology and behavior of people? What role does it play in the genesis of narcissism? It would be easy to say that power goes to one's head, inflating one's ego and turning one into a narcissist. But that is not the way narcissism develops. It grows out of the denial of feeling, the loss of self, and the projection of an image to compensate for that loss. In what way does power further that process? To understand that, we must start with the observation that power has a seemingly irresistible allure. Almost everyone wants power.

The most obvious advantage to having power is the material reward that accrues to the person with power. The king usually lives in a palace, the president of a country in a magnificent house, and the head of a large company in a mansion. In every way, their standard of living is superior to that of the average person. And they command the services of others to do the routine chores that most of us have to do ourselves. There is no question about the fact that power brings with it many material prerogatives, which are an important consideration in the desire for power. But they are not its most basic feature.

The struggle for power is not always between the haves and the have-nots. In feudal times, most wars were fought by a king who lived in one castle against a king who lived in another. Since, for the most part, each of these kings had all the material comforts and conveniences available, material need cannot be regarded as the major factor leading to the wars. Wars were waged by rulers to increase their domain and extend their control—in other words, to enlarge their power. True, victory did increase the winner's possessions and his wealth, but these were more important as symbols of power or as a means of power than as objects that directly added to comfort or pleasure. How many jewels a monarch wears bears no relation to human needs. Why, then, can't he or she have enough? In the final analysis, jewels are status symbols, which is true of so much of our wealth. The limousine an executive rides in may be more comfortable than an ordinary car, but it is also vastly more prestigious. A palace is really more a showplace than a home.

Power confers status. Isn't that a valid objective? We are all status seekers, and so are many other animals. Among chickens in the barnyard, there is a pecking order, reflecting the status of each hen. Status plays an important role in regulating relations among all animals that live in groups such as flocks or hunting packs. In such groups, a hierarchy is quickly established among the individual members. Status or position in the hierarchy determines precedence in the two most important functions in animal life: access to food and to mating. Translated into human terms, this means that the king would get the best food and the fairest lady, which was in fact the practice in the past. Among animals, this system has a definite survival value for the species, for it ensures the reproduction of the strongest and best-adapted members. One might speculate that a similar system operated in early human societies. Presumably, the chiefs would have been the strongest, bravest, and wisest, possessing qualities that would promote the welfare of their people. If their mates also possessed these qualities, their offspring would, in most likelihood, inherit them.

But these considerations are biological, not psychological. Neither a king nor a queen is thinking about the survival of the fittest in their amorous activities. Their attraction to each other is physical, and their motivation is the pleasure to be derived from their mating, not the product of that activity. Or that is what one might like to think. As it is, or rather was, kings did not marry for pleasure as much as for power, and royal sex was often charged with the need to produce an heir. But there was a time when kings were the strongest and bravest and queens the fairest in the land, at least according to our myths and fairy tales. The fairest lady holds out a promise of greater sexual pleasure for the man, just as the strongest and bravest man holds out a similar promise to the woman. These are not false promises when they are based on the bodily reality of the persons. Biologically, the status of an individual is represented by his or her sexual potency, which is an expression of the individual's vitality and energy. In nature, as opposed to culture, no one possesses power.

Originally, then, status led to power. But once power entered the human situation, that relationship became reversed. Power created status. The association of status with power extended the image of sexual potency to persons with power. This explains why so many women are sexually excited by and attracted to men with power. There would be no problem if power belonged to the superior individual. But that is not generally the case today. The reverse is often true. The man who needs and seeks power is in most cases relatively impotent sexually. Power is his way to compensate a lack of sexual potency. The question that arises is: How do women fit into this scheme? Do women narcissists seek power to compensate for some sense of sexual inadequacy? Yes. Power is the antidote to feelings of inadequacy and insensitivity on both the personal and the sexual levels, and women are as subject to these feelings as men. Like any man, they can strive for power in the worlds of business, politics, sports, etc. I am talking here about the need for and the striving for power. But power can also be acquired by a woman because of her superior abilities in any field of activity. Would this enhance her sexual appeal as it does in the case of a man? It should since psychologically, power is equated with superiority, which, on a physical level, translates into more energy and vitality. However, many men are frightened of women with power and so their sexual appeal would be limited to men who considered themselves their equal. In the past, power had generally been reserved for men, forcing many women to use their sexual charms to gain power, often considerable power. Thus, I might venture to say that in the case of men, power equals sexual potency, whereas in the case of women, sexual appeal equals power.

In my opinion, it is a mistake to believe that the psychology and the behavior of men and women are congruent. Few women that I know or have treated ever complained about their inability to satisfy a man sexually as some men do about their inability to satisfy a woman, that is, bring her to climax. On the other hand, few men feel used when they engage in sex with a woman. Men can't have sex without a strong desire manifested in an erection, while women can engage in sex with minimum feelings. Their bodies are different. Women's bodies tend to be softer, in consequence of which they tend to be more in touch with their feelings. However, this seems to be changing as women go in for body building in the same fashion as men. As they seek to present an image of strength and power, they become rigid, less sensitive, and more narcissistic. The world of unisex is a world without differences and, therefore, a world without feelings.

Generally speaking, the degree of narcissism is inversely proportional to sexual potency. But to understand this statement, we must recognize, again, the tie of sexual potency to feeling. For the man, sexual potency is not measured by the frequency of sexual activity or by his erective potency. Frequent sexual activity may be compulsive, stemming from a need for reassurance, or it may be impulsive, stemming from an inability to contain the sexual excitation. Erective potency—the ability to maintain an erection for an extended period of time during intercourse—may be a power maneuver. In effect, the man may say to the woman in body language: "See how powerful I am. Look what I can do for you." His focus is on power, represented by his ability to satisfy a woman. Unfortunately, this focus is at the expense of his own pleasure and fulfillment. What it denotes is the typically narcissistic need for approval and admiration. Nor, in the end, is the woman fulfilled. True sexual potency is measured by the depth of one's feeling of love for the other person. These feelings are greatly reduced in narcissists.

THE RELATIONSHIP TO ENVY AND RAGE

As we have seen, the symbolic identification of power with sexual potency underlies the great allure of power. That identification enables us to understand a number of reactions to power. Why is it, for instance, that those who play the power game never seem to feel that they have enough power? To answer that question, we must recognize that while the identification is valid on the ego level, it is an illusion on the bodily level. Power can energize the image, but it does nothing for the self and feelings. In fact, as we have seen, an overinvestment in the image weakens the self. By the same token, an overinvestment of energy in the struggle for power reduces the amount available for sexual pleasure. Misguided about the true source of sexual potency, the person seeks more power.

The equation of power with sexual potency also sheds light on why powerlessness is experienced with such humiliation. On some level of the personality, the feeling of being powerless is equivalent to being castrated, to use the male analogy. Very frequently a person whose power is threatened reacts to that threat as if it were a threat of castration. Both envy and rage can be related to this idea.

An important aspect of the nature of power is the envy it evokes in others. Power seems to confer on its possessor a mantle of superiority, specialness, and sexual potency, which the envious person desperately wants because he feels himself on some level to be inferior, unimportant, and impotent. If power evokes envy, it creates fear and leads to hostility. One tends to distrust the person with power because one feels vulnerable in the face of power. On the other hand, the person with power must distrust those who lack it because of their envy. Where power is great, one can easily become paranoid. The saying "Uneasy lies the head that wears the crown" reflects an ancient wisdom. Every person with power is vulnerable to the machinations of those who want that power. History is replete with plots to overthrow rulers. Rulers must be constantly on the alert to this danger. They can never be absolutely sure who their friends are.

Envy is not love. The person with power is feared and so cannot be loved. It is true that people sometimes pretend to love those they are afraid of and may even believe they do love them, but such love is usually based on a denial of the underlying fear and hatred. My patients, for instance, often claim to love their parents at the beginning of therapy. Then, as they come to realize how frightened they were of a parent, this sentiment disappears, to be replaced by a real anger. The emotions of love and fear are mutually exclusive. Not to fear a person with power—to profess, instead, one's love—is to deny that that person has power.

The emotion correlated with fear is anger. But narcissists are as incapable of expressing anger or feeling anger as they are of any other feeling. It is true that narcissists can and do at times fly into a rage. Indeed, one could say that a tendency to fits of rage is characteristic of this disturbance.

Isn't rage the same as anger? Although there is a strong

element of anger in an outburst of rage, the two expressions are not identical. Rage has an irrational quality—just think of the phrase "a blind rage." Anger, in contrast, is a focused reaction; it is directed toward removing a force that is acting against the person. When the force is removed or nullified, the anger subsides. A good example is the anger children feel when their movements are forcibly restrained. As soon as they are set free, their anger disappears. As adults, we may become angry for similar insults to our being. But true anger remains proportional to the provocation; it is a rational response to an attack. Thus, a verbal insult does not immediately lead to a fistfight, and the anger recedes after an apology. With a physical assault, we may want to return the injury, but the extent of this response is measured by the degree of actual danger.

Rage, however, is not in line with the provocation; it is excessive. Nor does rage subside with removal of the provocation; it continues until it is spent. And rage is destructive rather than constructive. Indeed, rage is tinged with a murderous intent. One of James Masterson's patients provides a clue to the meaning of rage. In this patient's words: "Giving up the idea of you and others doing it for me—leaves me feeling hopeless, helpless, and in a rage."[1] He then spoke of the feeling of wanting to kill. "When I have to do it myself, I feel thwarted and want to kill."

The incongruity of the reaction makes one suspect that the true motivation for the murderous intent was for a more serious insult or injury that had occurred earlier in life, probably in childhood, which was then repressed. If the repression was lifted and the injury made conscious, the reaction would change from one of rage to anger. That is the therapeutic task.

It is significant that an outburst of narcissistic rage be closely tied to the experience of frustration, of not being able to get one's way; in other words, of feeling powerless. For Masterson's patient, the frustration of not being able to get others to do it for him led to the rage reaction. Another of Masterson's patients flew into a rage because he did not respond to her wish to be treated as special. The frustration makes the person feel powerless and underscores the illusion of power associated with being special. When the illusion collapses, the rage associated with the original betrayal—a more significant insult that had occurred in early childhood to which one could not respond at that time—surfaces like the explosion of a volcano. But since it is divorced from an understanding of its source, in other words, since it is blind, it is ineffective as a remedy for the injury.

Why is this reaction called narcissistic rage? Recognizing the murderous quality to all such reactions, we can postulate that the insult provoking the reaction must strike a vital cord. The current provocation may be slight, as in the case of Masterson's patient, but the provocation evokes in the person's unconscious the memory of an earlier insult to which he or she could not respond when it occurred. Describing the rage as narcissistic tells us that the insult was to the person's sense of self, that it was a narcissistic injury. The experience was one of humiliation, of being powerless.

As we have seen, it is this experience of humiliation that underlies narcissists' striving for power. Through power, they believe that they can wipe out the insult. Any challenge to their power or image threatens to make them feel powerless and evokes the fear of being humiliated. Masterson's patient said that he felt "hopeless, helpless." It is difficult to see how such feelings could send someone into a rage. They would seem more likely to lead to a feeling of despair. But if we change this patient's words to "feeling powerless," his reaction makes sense. Like so many narcissistic patients, he was in a power struggle with his therapist, and he believed that he had control of the situation. The shock of finding that he was really powerless triggered a rage that was both irrational and murderous.

The Case of David

A patient of mine, David, began by describing his reaction of rage when his son had persisted in an action he had been told to stop. The boy kept jumping on the bed where his father and younger brother were lying. David was afraid that the boy's jumping would injure the child. David didn't think he was wrong in ordering the boy to stop. What bothered him was the recognition that his reaction of rage was excessive. As he explained it, "I realized the enormity of my rage when I saw the look of fear in my son's face. I thought that he was afraid I could kill him, and I sensed that there was a murderous quality in my tone of voice and in my look."

David was aware that his rage reaction was triggered by his son's disobedience which left him feeling frustrated. It was as if the boy's disobedience was a challenge to his power. But why did David react so strongly? What was the real source of his rage? He said, "I saw that I was doing to my son what my father had done to me. I was a frightened kid, but until recently I denied I was afraid. I had moments of fear. I was a college wrestler, and I was always afraid before the match. I was afraid that I wouldn't be strong enough, powerful enough. I was afraid I would lose, but I always won."

On some level, winning or losing had the connotation of life or death. Each fight was like a battle in war. Then David added, "I did lose one match, the finals of the state tournament. I could have been the champ, but I didn't have the killer instinct." But David really is a killer. His rage has a murderous quality. Just because he really can kill, he dare not make a total effort, for that might lead to real killing. He doesn't have the killer instinct, as he put it, because he has the killer intent.

David then reflected on his preoccupation with winning:

"I'm a performer, and I need to win. Watching sports, I root for the underdog, but he must win. I have a big fear of losing. Losing would be failure, death. If I have no power, I'm dead. I need power. I go through life pitting my power against others. If they win, I'm dead—that's just a feeling, not the actuality. Yet I ended my wrestling career with the sense that I disappointed my coaches and myself. If I had worked at it, I could have been national or intercollegiate champ. Sports were a life-and-death struggle for me. I was afraid of losing."

It was obvious to me that David was fighting against himself. On a feeling level—inside—he was scared to death. Yet on an ego level—in terms of outward appearance—he was strong and powerful. That was the image he projected with his muscular body and his successful career as a surgeon. David operated on cases that might frighten others. He denied any fears and exuded self-confidence.

David had developed this image in his youth. He explained that he had tried to be the kind of kid a parent would love, a model son—smart, athletic, good-looking, well behaved. But did he feel he was that? What was going on inside?

"As a kid, I was scared a lot," David admitted. "I was afraid of the dark and of being alone. I couldn't go to sleep unless my brother lay in bed with me. I'm still that way. I can't stand being alone for more than fifteen minutes."

When I asked David who had scared him as a child, he didn't know. But then he mentioned that his father used to beat him with a strap and that his mother hit him with a shoe. As he now recollected: "I used to have nightmares, and my father would slap me to wake me up. I used to be sent to my room, and I wanted to kill myself to get even. I never acknowledged my fear until this year. Now my dreams are full of fear. I feel fear in relation to women and sex. I'm afraid I won't be able to perform. I never acknowledged that fear before. What frightens me most is when I do not have control over a situation. I am scared of illness."

Masterson explains the self-destructive tendency associated with the rage (David's wish to kill himself rather than his father) as the "attempt to master it (the rage) by internalizing it, using the mechanism of identification with the aggressor. . . . He discharges the rage by attacking himself, fantasying revenge on the parents and fulfillment of his talionic impulses by destroying their possession."[2] While this is psychologically true, I don't believe it goes deep enough. Self-destructive behavior is always determined by an underlying sense of guilt. This guilt stems from the Oedipal situation. David can accept his desire to kill his father in retaliation for the beating he received from him, but to kill his father is an admission of sexual desire for the mother, and this admission is under the strong taboo against being a "mother fucker." Out of this guilt he identified with his father. But now he is a real father, which permits him to project upon his own son the forbidden sexual feelings. The son's disobedience is reacted to unconsciously as a threat to kill the father, which must be met by an attack in kind.

At this point, David commented, "In my work I feel powerful. I'm like a stone face. It would take a tragedy to make me feel deeply."

David's account clearly reveals the role that power plays in compensating for inner feelings of fear, humiliation, and helplessness. Yet David had not fully connected his own fear with his father, despite his recognition that a child reacts to a parent's rage with great fear. For a parent to rage at a child is inhuman. But humanness is alien to the narcissist. David said of himself, "I can be a hero or a coward. I don't know any in-between." The in-between is to be human, which is to accept one's helplessness in life, recognize one's dependence on others, and admit one's failures and wrongs.

THE FEAR OF HELPLESSNESS

Power can be countered only with power, so the battle becomes endless. It is no answer for the powerless to demand equal power. There is no such thing as equal power. If everyone had equal power, no one could control anyone else. That means there would be no real power. Once you think in terms of power, there is only the struggle for more power. No one ever has enough power. Power will not overcome one's inferiority, ease an inner feeling of humiliation, or provide orgastic potency. Power serves only to deny these feelings. By its very nature, then, power increases the person's narcissism and reinforces the underlying insecurity.

In many ways, power is a denial of one's humanity. As we have seen, through power the narcissist attempts to transcend feelings of helplessness and dependency. But isn't a certain helplessness part of the human condition? We don't ask to be born, in general, and we have no say over when we will die. We cannot choose with whom to fall in love. There are many instances in which we are not the masters of our fate. Yet our helplessness in these areas is tolerable because all human beings are in the same boat. And we need each other to counter the darkness, to keep out the cold, to provide meaning to existence. Human beings are social creatures. It is with other people that we find the warmth, the excitement, and the challenge of life. And only within the human community do we dare face the frightening unknown.

Narcissists are not exceptions to this human need. They, too, need people. But they dare not acknowledge this need. To do so is to admit and face their vulnerability. Asking for help would be opening the narcissistic wound suffered as a child when, helpless and dependent, one was used by the parent who had power. Being in need and being helpless seem to allow the other person to control one's fate. Since one is helpless and does have needs—despite one's denial—one finds the solution in gaining sufficient power (money, for example) so that one can buy or command what one needs without risking the danger of rejection or seduction.

Power, or so the narcissist thinks, allows one to gain human contact without the danger of being used. With power, one can attract others. For the less disturbed narcissistic character, power rests in the use of his or her charm, wit, and good looks to lure admirers. Psychopathic personalities, on the other hand, tend to use the power of wealth or position to amass followers, or they may be overtly seductive. They know all too well how to play on the fears and weaknesses of others, for they, too, have these fears. Thus, they promise and proclaim that they will be the light and the security other people seek. In their own minds, they hold themselves out as superior, believing they don't need anyone. And they often seem superior because human anxieties do not plague them. Desperate, frightened, and lost people turn to them as saviors. Haven't they demonstrated that they are above the human struggle? But even if the psychopathic personality doesn't acquire a flock of followers, he or she must have at least one devotee, whether a lover or a prostitute. In other words, psychopathic personalities must have someone who needs them. They cannot be alone. And the relationship must be one in which they have control.

The issue of power and control also enters into the therapeutic situation. No basic change in personality or character can occur if the patient is in control of the therapy. But most narcissistic patients are terrified of surrendering control. They do not fully trust the therapist—and given their early-life experiences, this is understandable. They are afraid of being used, as they were in their families. They see the therapist as having power, which they resent and resist. This is, of course, a transference problem. Much as they need help, they cannot fully accept their dependency on another to help them change their condition. To be powerless is too humiliating. One must remain in control.

Control is maintained by denying and suppressing feeling. Yet the therapeutic endeavor aims at helping patients open up to and accept their feelings. That means that patients must learn to give up control. They must learn to let their feelings and emotions move them, even allowing themselves to be carried away by their emotional responses—otherwise they will never know the glory of love and the exuberance of joy. But here is the dilemma: It is just this fear of being carried away by feeling that frightens narcissists. It raises a fear of insanity, against which they will mobilize all their defenses. In these patients' minds, to lose control of oneself is equated with going crazy.

However, before we consider this aspect of the narcissistic problem, we need to examine in more detail the seductive process that produces in narcissists a sense of betrayal. To be rejected or openly hurt evokes a feeling of anger, but to be betrayed by a false promise from a trusted person arouses a murderous rage.

5

Seduction and Manipulation

CLEARLY, narcissists need power to inflate their self-image, which would collapse like an empty balloon without it. But how does one develop such a grandiose image of oneself? I have already discarded the hypothesis that it is a carry-over from a state of primary narcissism, or infantile omnipotence. Infants are without guile (the innocence of babes), and they react spontaneously, based on the bodily self's needs. What happens to destroy this innocence—and even more, to rob one of one's bodily self and to place one in the special position of feeling superior? The sequence of events follows a definite order. First comes the humiliating experience of powerlessness (see Chapter 4). Then comes a process of seduction, by which the child is made to see him- or herself as special. An additional element, usually accompanying humiliation, is rejection. After being rejected and humiliated, a child is more easily seduced into serving the parent.

What do I mean by seduction? The word "seduction" comes from the Latin *seducere*, "to lead aside." We speak of people who are seduced into abandoning their faith, principles, or allegiance. They are led aside from the straight and narrow path of virtue, which ultimately means to be true to oneself, to one's deepest feelings. We describe a man as seducing a woman if, knowing it runs against her principles to engage in sex without love, he lures her into a sexual relationship by professing a love he does not feel. Obviously a man would not need to seduce a woman who simply desired a sexual relationship, with or without love. Seduction may therefore be defined as the use of a false statement or promise to get another person to do what he or she would not otherwise do.

The promise can be explicitly stated, or it can be implied. Psychopathic swindlers openly promise something they have no intention of giving. But most seductive ploys involve promises that are not clearly stated. The narcissistic image is an example. If we look at the macho male, with his exaggerated show of virility, we realize that he is being seductive whether he admits it or not. Although his image arose as a compensation for an inadequate sense of his male self, it is intended to attract women. By emphasizing "manly" strength, it implies sexual potency, thus holding out a promise of sexual fulfillment to a woman. But the promise is false, as we have seen, because the image belies the reality. Any man who is dependent on an image to attract a woman is not sexually potent.

An important element in the seduction process is the nature of the relationship in which it takes place. Seduction is not a marketplace transaction, in which both parties are equal and the rule of caveat emptor applies. A shrewd trade is not considered a swindle or a seduction. Seduction occurs only in relationships in which some degree of trust exists. Swindlers are called con artists because they first gain their victims' confidence. To lead someone astray, you must first get him or her to trust you. Seduction, therefore, is always a betrayal. And this betrayal is all the more pernicious in the parent-child relationship, in which trust is basic.

THE MAKING OF PRINCE CHARMING

Steven, a young man I knew, projected an image of himself as "Prince Charming." His charm was turned on automatically whenever he was in the company of a woman. His good-looking face took on an easy smile, and his wit came out in engaging repartees. In contrast, when his charm was turned off, he looked dejected, and one could sense that he was insecure and frightened. Unfortunately, if a young woman responded to his charm, believing that it offered the promise of an exciting relationship, she was sadly disappointed. His engaging manner vanished as soon as the seduction ended, even if it was successful. He did not have the energy to maintain the façade indefinitely.

Steven's charm was not only turned on to further sexual interests. He also used it to make friends, to impress people and get them to support him. Through this image, he denied his dependency and at the same time seduced others into being there for him. It was a power play, as is every seductive maneuver.

The Prince Charming look was a pose that Steven had adopted. He wasn't born that way. Because I knew his family, I had observed the development of this role in Steven's interactions with his parents as a boy. In his childhood, I saw that when he played the Prince Charming role, his mother smiled at him. It pleased and excited her—obviously, he was her Prince Charming. His father, on the other hand, seemed embarrassed by the boy's behavior and became angry with him. It was clear to me that Steven's father resented the special relationship the boy had with his mother.

A situation like this only develops when the relationship between the parents is unfulfilling. Wanting something from her husband that he cannot give her, the mother turns to her son for it. I would guess that it is the excitement of romance. This is the promise that Prince Charming makes, though he cannot fulfill it. But what is the inducement the mother offers her son to get him to play this role for her?

The inducement is the offer of a special relationship with mother, carrying a promise of closeness and intimacy. For the child, the promise of closeness is particularly compelling because he was deprived of it in infancy. If his mother had been "there" for him then, he would not be so ready now to make a deal sacrificing the self for a promise. But having been rejected earlier, the boy is anxious for acceptance now. And the timing of "now" is important. The promise is made when the boy is between the ages of three and six—old enough to comprehend the demand made on him but not independent enough to be able to reject it. Moreover, this is the time of the Oedipal period, when the child's interest in the parent of the opposite sex is strongly sexual. The proffered intimacy takes on a sexual nuance. In actuality, the boy may be allowed to watch his mother dress or even to assist her in her toilet. She may share private feelings and thoughts with him, treating him as her confidant. There are many subtle ways a mother can excite her son sexually and so tie him to her. The tie becomes even stronger if he is made to feel guilty for his responsiveness.

The idea of being in a special relationship with his mother has many meanings for the boy. (And everything I say here about the boy's special relationship with his mother generally applies to the girl in a special relationship with her father.) It always means to be the preferred one. In Steven's case, it meant: "Mother loves me more than my brother or my father. Therefore, I am superior to them." The boy also senses from the situation that he is needed by his mother. What a sense of importance that must give a child! How could one not develop a grandiose self-image under these conditions? Who would want to avoid the illusion of power (to be the only one who can fulfill a parent) that the situation provides?

Peter, a patient of mine, was repeatedly told by his mother, when he was small, that he was God's child. She was a very religious woman and very controlling. If he uttered a "dirty" word, his mouth was washed with soap. On the one hand, he was not spared humiliation, but on the other, he was made to feel special. Peter was a handsome young man, but I sensed in him an agony, which I associated with the crucifixion of Christ. At times his face took on a Christ-like expression of suffering and resignation. And he did suffer—from a narcissistic disturbance. He was depressed, with little feeling, and his sexual potency was reduced. Fortunately, through our work, Peter was able to recognize the degree to which he had been made to feel special. He was able to cry and to feel the sadness of the loss of the self. And after he had mourned this loss, his Christ-like expression changed to one of aliveness and presence. It was almost as if he had returned from the dead. As I saw it, his mother had needed him to be Christ-like so she could raise her sexuality to a spiritual level. In the process, Peter's sexuality was sacrificed.

THE MEANING OF SPECIALNESS

The promise of specialness is the seductive lure put forward in the parent's effort to mold the child into his or her image of what the child should be. In most cases, the promise is not explicit but implicit in the parent's attitude toward the child, which the child clearly senses.

In American culture, most parents want something or seem to need something from their children. For some parents, a child has to be successful in the world, often to compensate for the parent's own sense of failure. For others, the child has to be outstanding, to achieve some recognition that will make the parent feel important. Too often, parents turn to their children for the affection and support they did not receive from their own parents and are not getting from their spouses. It seems, too, that many parents have a need to be superior to their children—to make up for the inferiority they felt when they were young and from which they still suffer unconsciously. Parents tend to identify with their children and to project onto them their own unfulfilled longings and desires.

For their part, children want to be free—free to grow up according to their own natures. They expect the parent to be there for them, not the reverse. With the parent placing demands on the child and the child making demands on the parent, a situation of conflict quickly develops. In Chapter 4, we saw how this conflict develops into a power struggle between parent and child. Parents do have sufficient physical force to break a child's will, and many take advantage of this "power." But this tactic also generates hostility and an underlying rebellion in the child, which will defeat the parent in the end. Actually, a parent's most potent weapon is rejection, or the threat of it. Since children are completely dependent on their parents, they cannot resist this threat. And, of course, there is seduction, a tactic that usually comes later, when the child's ego has developed to a point where it can comprehend the deal.

Again, the deal is that the child will be treated or regarded as "special" if he or she submits to the parent. Every narcissistic individual I have encountered "feels" special. I put the word "feel" in quotes because specialness is not a body sensation but a mental construct. It is, therefore, a matter of belief or thinking rather than a feeling. Nevertheless, the person who "feels" superior does translate this onto the body level, through the ego's dissociating from the body and sensing itself above the body.

Being special colors the image, taking it beyond the range of "commonness." However, the values associated with the image are illusory; there is no real superiority or strength in an image. Real virtues lie with the inner being, with the humanity of the person, not with his image. There is nothing special about being human; it is the common if not the average condition of people. And we shall see when we compare the qualities associated with "specialness" and "commonness" that the real advantages lie with the latter.

Let us start with what it means to be special. I often pose this question to my narcissistic patients. Each has his or her own unique image. One woman said, "I always thought I was special. I was told I could achieve anything I wanted if I tried hard enough, and I believed it. Isn't that the American Way?" Then she added, "I achieved a lot, but it didn't work in the important area of love and sex." Another patient declared, "It means people will point me out and look up to me. They will admire me." A psychiatrist answered, "For me, being special means knowing all the secrets of people's lives. I sit behind the scenes like a director or producer knowing everything that's going to happen." In the musical *The Fantasticks*, the ingenue sings a song about her wish to be "special." She doesn't spell out what she means, but one can imagine that "specialness" represents her desire to be worshiped, to be loved as a goddess.

What are the qualities highlighted by these people? A simple listing includes (1) "I can do anything" (omnipotence), (2) "I am visible everywhere" (omnipresence), (3) "I know everything" (omniscience), and (4) "I am to be worshiped." These, of course, are the attributes of a god. On some deep level, narcissists, and especially psychopathic personalities, see themselves as little gods. Too often, unfortunately, their followers look up to them in that light, too.

But how does one come to think oneself a god? As I have indicated, specialness denotes a special relationship to the parent, one of greater intimacy. The child is allowed to share some of the parent's problems and desires. There may also be a closer physical intimacy—for instance, rubbing father's back or helping mother dress. The proffered intimacy and the sense of being special are quite compelling to a child who has felt rejected, even if that intimacy requires moving into the parent's world and giving up one's freedom. Rejection is an intolerable situation for a child. In itself, the frustrated longing for love is extremely painful. But the consequent sense of being unlovable and the conclusion that it must be due to some fault or failure in oneself is devastating. The child sees no way out of this impossible position other than to accept the offer of specialness and intimacy. Acceptance amounts to almost total identification with the rejecting parent—an identification that represents the fusion of the self-image with the parental image as conceived by psychoanalytic writers. It is, however, a secondary development occurring after some separation has occurred. Its effect raises the child's ego to super-normal heights, inflating it to such a degree that it seems superhuman. Since the parent is god-like to a young child, this fusion of images endows the child's ego with a similar quality.

This kind of identification with the parent splits the child's identity. Through it, the child incorporates the parent's values wholesale and develops a self-image to reflect them. At the same time, the child must reject the self that the parent found objectionable—namely, bodily feelings and the desire to be independent. In this process, the parent's values become superior to those values associated with the body and its feelings. To be special is therefore to be superior to one's bodily self. The child comes to believe that what the parent rejected was only the child's "lower" nature. This illusion assuages the pain, which is then denied. The child's new self-image acquires status as an expression of his or her "higher" nature.

Obviously, "higher" and "lower" nature refer to the mind

and the body, respectively. "It was only my body and its feelings that were rejected," these children tell themselves. With their minds, the children conclude, they can transcend that inferior way of being and become a superior person, like mother or father. With their minds, they can gain control and suppress those feelings which are unacceptable and cause pain. They thus suppress and deny their disappointment at the rejection of bodily needs, their fear of the parent, their anger at the earlier use of force, and their sadness and despair over the loss of true love. Through the new self-image, they compensate for the sense of unlovableness and unworthiness that they previously experienced.

To be superior is to be above it—meaning above the body and its "lower" nature. The person or the self is in the head, energetically speaking, rather than in the body. Energy or libido is invested in the ego and focused on the image the person is projecting. "Feeling" special and superior, thinking oneself above the body, and disclaiming or denying feeling compose the characterological attitude of the narcissist.

The denial of feeling applies particularly to the sexual feelings. "Lower" nature refers directly to the lower part of the body and its functions. Defecation, urination, and sexuality are stigmatized as dirty. Often, in my opinion, the disclaimer has its roots in the mother's rejection of her own body and its animal nature, which is then extended to the child's body. In my view, that rejection is manifested in the mother's rejection of breast-feeding, which helps to bond the mother and the infant in a naturally close relationship. Breast-feeding may, unconsciously, be regarded by some women as too sexual and therefore dirty. Such women are ashamed to be seen breast-feeding a child.

But to disclaim sexual feeling doesn't mean it disappears. Although the relationship between the seducing parent and the child may be nonsexual or even antisexual on the surface, the intimacy that develops between them has a sexual nuance.

The Case of Martha

Martha was in her late thirties when she consulted me because of a lack of feeling. She described a kind of deadness that made her feel strange, somewhat unreal. Yet an observer might have had difficulty seeing her deadness or strangeness. She seemed to function like a normal person and did not appear depressed. She held a good job and got along reasonably well with her employer and fellow workers, at least on the job. Away from work, she had little contact with any of them. Indeed, apart from her job, she complained her life was empty. She did not have a relationship with a man, nor did she have any desire for such a relationship. And how could she be close to women when their talk turned to men? The subject was an alien world to her. In the presence of other women, then, she felt her strangeness. So she went to work, came home, took care of her needs, and prepared for the next day's work. Martha felt the emptiness of her life but said she had no energy for anything else.

As I noted, it wasn't easy to see Martha's deadness—at least at first glance. It was covered up by a seemingly vivacious manner. She smiled, laughed, and chattered as if everything were all right. She didn't cry, nor did she show sadness or any other feeling.

As we worked, Martha developed a very positive feeling for me. She claimed it was because I could see her deadness, sense the emptiness of her life, and empathize with her unexpressed sadness. I was a real human being, in her view. Moreover, through our bioenergetic body work, Martha began to gain some feeling in her body, and this affected the transference.

Breathing, kicking, and grounding exercises promoted vibrations in her legs, which she could feel.[1] Intense work on the tense muscles of her throat opened her voice. Martha's jaw muscles were also constricted and needed considerable work. Her jaw was set in an attitude of grim determination: *Do not feel anything.* Eventually, through this work, Martha became able to cry—a major breakthrough for her. She realized that she needed to cry and often asked me to work on her jaw so she could cry. But this was the only feeling she could muster for a long time.

If crying is such a basic function, how do we lose it? Why do so many patients have difficulty in crying? A baby's crying is also a call to a parent, for while it may release the tension, the crying does not remove the cause of the tension, which, in most cases, is a need for contact with a parent. If that loving contact is not forthcoming, the tension will persist and the crying will continue. There is, however, a limit to a child's ability to cry. It can cry itself out, as we say. At this point, it has no more energy to sustain the crying, and so it stops or falls asleep exhausted. To continue beyond this point would risk death, since the child would have to call upon energy that is needed to maintain vital functions. This experience is highly traumatic, since it creates an association in the child's mind between deep crying and death. Many of my patients have experienced this connection as they allow themselves to feel their despair and cry from the depth of their being. But to achieve such a breakthrough, one has to work through a great unconscious resistance stemming from the fear of death. That resistance is largely structured in chronic muscular tensions about the throat which prevent deep sobbing and so, seemingly, serve to guard life. One also finds severe tensions in the muscles of the chest wall which block deep crying and serve, unconsciously, to protect the person against the pain in his or her heart.

It may seem that the goal of bioenergetic analysis is to get patients to cry. This isn't so. The goal may be described as the attainment of selfhood, which comprises self-awareness, self-expression, and self-possession. Being aware of oneself means being fully in touch with the body, but that is possible only if the person gains insight into the unconscious motivations of behavior. Self-expression denotes the ability to sense and express all feelings, while self-possession means that one is in conscious command of this expression. Every chronic muscular tension blocks all three functions. The body work aims at helping a person feel this blockage, understand it, and release it. This is a continuous process, since the release of tension occurs gradually as the organism learns to tolerate and integrate the higher levels of excitation associated with more intense feelings. Crying, that is, sobbing is the earliest and deepest way to release tension. Infants can cry almost from the moment of birth, and do so easily following every stress that produces a state of tension in the body. One moment the baby's body is tense, the next its jaw quivers, and then it breaks down into a convulsive release of the tension. Human beings are the only creatures who can react in this way to stress and tension. Most probably, they are the only ones who need this form of release.

We must also recognize that crying is not generally acceptable by parents. It often annoys them, to say the least, especially when it persists despite their efforts to calm the child. Some parents believe that to respond to a crying child gives the child control over the parents. They see the issue as one of power. Other parents are out of touch with the true needs of the child and do not know how to respond. One parent told me that as he was walking and holding his crying baby in the middle of the night, he could easily have thrown it out of the window, he was so angry. Can we imagine that a baby is insensitive to this feeling, that it isn't aware that by crying it risks the loss of the love it needs? Other parents are more openly hostile, telling a crying child that if it doesnt stop, they will give it something to cry about. And they do hit it to stop its crying. What child can continue to cry in the face of such a response? Then there are the parents who impress upon a child the idea that no one will love it unless it smiles. It doesn't surprise me that my patients have difficulty crying. I did.

But some patients say, "Crying is no problem for me. I cry easily. In fact, I cry too much, and it doesn't seem to help me." Such a statement is only partly true. Some people cry when they should be angry, and their crying can be seen as a defense against their anger. Crying is not the only feeling that one needs to be able to express. Still, I don't believe there is such a thing as "crying too much." The fact that the crying persists means that there is a continuing state of tension in the body. And because of that tension, a continuing state of sadness. I explain to these persons that they are crying off the top of their sadness, that the crying is not deep enough to empty their barrel of tears nor to fully release the tension. It's not how much one cries but how deeply one cries which determines the release. Most patients accept this explanation and realize that they have to open up more.

Let us return to Martha's case. The story she told was one of rejection and humiliation. She described her mother as a cold, unfeeling woman. Martha couldn't remember any contact with her mother as a child. She had been born in Europe during the war and was in fact separated from her mother in her early years. What she did recall were her constant efforts as a child to make some contact with her brother, who was two years older. He, however, pushed her away or ignored her, as if she didn't exist. Although Martha emphasized the painfulness of these experiences, her voice was without feeling. She went on to describe how this treatment by her brother continued all through her childhood and into her adolescence. He refused to let his friends play with her and sometimes punched and hit her. When she told her mother about this treatment, she was instructed not to bother her brother. Her father's behavior to her was even crueler, though not physically violent. He never spoke to her, burying himself in a newspaper. If Martha approached him, he would turn to her mother and ask, "What does *she* want?" He always referred to her as "she"; he never called her by name.

In view of this treatment by the male members of her family, one could hardly expect Martha to have loving feelings for a man. And she didn't. In her early twenties, feeling the desperate need for physical contact with another human being, she had engaged in sexual activity with men. But she did so without sexual feeling. The contact didn't seem much, and she felt used by them so she stopped that practice. Yet Martha was troubled that she had absolutely no sexual desire. It contributed to her feeling of strangeness and unreality.

We both recognized that Martha had considerable hostility toward men, stemming from her experiences with her brother and her father. Because such hostility blocks any sexual desire, I had Martha express her anger against them many times in the course of her therapy. She also felt and expressed her contempt and disgust for her father, in retaliation for the disgust he showed toward her. Yet Martha was aware that as a child she had longed desperately for some contact with her brother and her father. I was reasonably certain that that longing had a sexual element. During the Oedipal period, a girl is attracted sexually to the male members of her family. In Martha, both the longing and sexual feeling for her father and her brother were strongly suppressed. If her hostility toward them was the force that kept these feelings in a state of suppression, the release of the hostility should allow them to surface. But this did not happen. I knew then that some other force must be operating to maintain the suppression.

The hostility shown toward Martha by her brother and her father could only be explained as a transference of the hostility they felt toward the mother. Unable to express it toward her, they vented it on Martha because she, too, was female. I could understand their rancor toward Martha's mother, a cold, unfeeling woman who found sex or anything sexual repulsive. In some way she must have humiliated the males (husband and son), and they in turn humiliated Martha. Though Martha could comprehend this, for she, too, was repulsed by her mother's stony lack of feeling, she could not feel any anger against her mother. Instead, she felt sorry for her.

Martha's relationship to her mother struck me as odd. They were on the telephone to each other regularly, speaking to each other in endearing terms, like lovers. Martha put on her "everything is all right" façade for her mother, just as she did for the world, and probably for the same reason: to deny and hide her feelings. Nevertheless, her behavior ran counter to the often-expressed repugnance she felt to the idea of any physical contact with her mother. I could only conclude that there was a secret tie between Martha and her mother, even though at first I did not understand it.

When all my therapeutic efforts to alleviate her sexual unresponsiveness proved of no avail, I began to realize that Martha was allied with her mother in an antisex stance against men. I then confronted Martha with this idea of an alliance, and she admitted that she identified with her mother's attitude of superiority to other people. Her mother had told her that "common" people were like animals who acted on their feelings. Martha and her mother were above that. They were special. Only after this pact was broken open could Martha feel the deep sadness at the loss of her sexuality and the anger against her mother for this loss. Expressing that anger, which was tinged with a murderous rage, paved the way for the breakthrough of her sexuality.

Expressing anger is not only a verbal act, for the anger is locked up in the body as muscular tension in the upper back between and around the shoulder blades. When Martha sensed the anger against her mother, she took the tennis racket, which is always available in bioenergetic therapy, and began to beat the bed with it. As she did this, she expressed in words her anger against her mother. "I hate you. I could kill you. You robbed me of my sexuality." She had done this exercise before expressing her anger about her suffering, but this time it was specifically directed against her mother with insight into its origin.

I see this kind of relationship between mother and daughter as homosexual in nature because the feelings expressed toward each other are those which are normally directed toward a person of the opposite sex. But what is the bond in this kind of homosexual relationship? What ties the daughter to her mother on a sexual level and vice versa? Each supports the other's antisex and antimale position by offering a pseudoaffection that negates the need for men. This kind of tie, however, is premised on "no" rather than "yes," what one is against rather than what one is for. It is a link between victims. A mother who feels victimized by men can easily seduce her daughter into an identification with that position. Similarly, a father who feels dominated by his wife can seduce his son into an alliance against "bitches" to justify his personal failure as a man.

But what happens if the seduction proceeds from mother to son, or father to daughter? In this case, the seduction carries the aura of incest. Sexual feelings must be denied because of guilt, as we can see in Mark's case.

The Case of Mark

Mark, a successful psychiatrist in his mid-forties, consulted me following the death of his son Donald, an only child, in an automobile accident. Donald, a young man of twenty, had been out with some friends drinking and was driving home alone when the accident occurred. Mark blamed himself somewhat for the tragedy because he had ignored evident signs that his son was in trouble. Before the accident, Mark was unaware that he, too, was in trouble of a different kind.

Mark had been married and divorced twice. Donald was a child of the first marriage. At present Mark was involved with another woman, but this relationship was also unsatisfactory. This woman complained, he said, that he didn't have much feeling. He began to think that perhaps this was true, because although he felt very upset about his son's death, he could not cry deeply about it. He could not really grieve.

Mark was an attractive man with a well-built, muscular body. Two features, however, struck me. They are important to note because a person is his or her body—that is, the expression of the body reveals the person's character. First of all, Mark's forehead was contracted and his brows were pulled downward, giving his eyes a searching, distrustful look. Had the contraction and knitting of the forehead been more severe, I would have characterized the look as paranoid. The second feature was evident only when Mark was undressed. He showed an extreme contraction around his pelvic area. Because such tension would allow little feeling into the pelvis, I surmised that Mark had some sexual difficulties. Mark, however, assured me that his penis functioned very well, that he had no problems with erective potency.

As we talked about the death of his son, Mark became able to cry about it. His sobbing, however, was neither deep nor sustained. Still, as Mark put it, "It represents a change. I haven't cried in decades. I prided myself on being the strong one—able to carry on and support others, to produce. I've always produced, but I feel now that it hasn't been a positive thing. I've never made my wives happy; I've never been happy. And I am in the same situation now with my girlfriend."

Why did Mark think that he had to be strong, always

producing? According to him, his father wasn't a producer, and his mother complained about it. "She had contempt for him, and I did, too," Mark commented. "It's not that he didn't work and earn a living, but he was not ambitious. I've achieved much more than he did."

When I asked Mark about his relationship with his mother, he replied, "I was very close to her. She confided in me, and I felt I was more her husband than my father. I felt I had to take care of her." The Oedipal situation, it seemed to me, must have been highly charged, so I questioned Mark about his sexual feelings for his mother. "I don't recall any," he answered. "My mother's attitude was that the lower part of the body was dirty." He remembered that as a child he used to lie in bed with his mother, but only their feet touched. On the other hand, as he related to me later, his mother used to give him enemas, which he found quite exciting.

Mark was a narcissistic character, and as we have seen, this personality structure does not experience guilt feelings in relation to sexuality. This doesn't mean that these feelings are absent. They are denied like other feelings, such as sadness and anger, and they are translated into a fear of failure in sexual performance. He was a psychiatrist, however, and so he could appreciate that the Oedipal situation which he had just described would necessarily lead to guilt feelings about sexuality. This was an intellectual realization. To feel his guilt, he needed a deeper contact with his sexuality.

In contrast to this closeness to his mother, Mark felt distant from his father. His sister, who was two years younger, was closer to his father. This kind of division of children—a boy for you, a girl for me—is common in my experience. Each child is seduced into a "special" intimacy with the parent of the opposite sex. The child's developing ego is highly flattered by this position and swells up with importance, making for a "swell head." At the same time, however, there is rivalry and competitiveness with the parent of the same sex, who reacts with anger against the child's presumption of superiority. And Mark recalled that his father sometimes looked at him with hostility. The parent's anger frightens the child, who is really helpless and dependent. But since one can't be superior if one is frightened, the fear is suppressed and denied. Mark claimed he was not afraid of his father.

As a child, then, Mark was in an Oedipal bind from which there was only one way out—namely, cutting off his sexual feelings for his mother. As Freud has pointed out, this move is taken under the threat of castration by the father.* Of course, this threat is not explicitly stated, but it is implicit in the father's attitude to the boy. At the same time, the mother rejects any sexual overtures by the boy, despite her covert seduction. Mark, for example, was encouraged to lie in bed with his mother, but only their feet were allowed to touch.

To cut off sexual feelings by chronic tension in the pelvic musculature, as Mark did, is in effect a psychological castration. Yet Mark denied the castration and pictured himself as a potent male—erectively potent, that is. He did not, however, experience the melting sensation of love, which, as we have seen, is crucial for true sexual satisfaction. By contracting and tightening his pelvis, Mark cut off sensation in the area around his penis, isolating that organ. Although Mark had full sensation in his penis, it was not connected to any feeling in the rest of his body. In other words, psychological castration means loss of sexual feeling in the body, especially the pelvis, while retaining sensation in the genitals. The effect is to limit the orgastic response. Even though he denied the castration, Mark was aware that some-

* Freud postulated that the threat of castration results in a positive resolution of the Oedipus conflict. I don't see it that way. In my view, the conflict is resolved temporarily at the expense of the child's sexuality.[2]

thing was amiss. In an earlier session, he had remarked that his penis did not feel as if it were part of him.

To regain sexual feeling in his pelvis, Mark had to sense the tension in that area and experience the fear of castration it represented. When the tension is extreme, as in Mark's case, any pressure on the muscles is painful. It is by feeling this pain that the person becomes aware of the tension and of the underlying fear. If the person can relax these muscles, the pain disappears and the pelvis becomes warm and suffused with feeling. The pressure I apply is rarely strong because most patients are frightened of being hurt in the pelvic area. Generally, if I make an unexpected movement either inadvertently or deliberately in that area, the patient will jump with fear. Yet experiencing that fear enables the person to realize that it must stem from earlier experiences, for the patient knows that I do not intend any harm. That realization allows the patient to relax under my pressure and experience the warmth and pleasure of pelvic sexuality.

To my surprise, Mark didn't react at all when I applied pressure with my fingers to the tight muscles in his groin. Even increasing the pressure elicited no response. He could feel the pressure, and there was some pain, he said, but he could take it. In fact, he told me, he felt like laughing at me. He suppressed the laugh because he sensed it had a diabolical ring. I asked Mark to go ahead and laugh. It came out "Ha, ha, ha," with a mocking tone as if to say: "You didn't get to me" or "You didn't frighten me."

I have heard such devilish laughs a number of times in the course of my work with patients. The laugh always has the same meaning, for it always breaks out just when it seems the patient should respond emotionally. A patient appears to be on the verge of tears, but instead of crying, this laugh occurs. An emotional response would show that the person has been affected by the experience. The laughter denies any feeling. "I won," it declares. "I am more powerful than you. I can resist you." Such laughter is one hallmark of narcissistic patients, for it represents a clear denial of feeling.

But why do we say such a laugh has a diabolical or devilish sound? This isn't only my description; everyone who hears the laugh senses that quality. And yet no one has actually heard a devil laugh. We don't believe in devils, at least the mythical kind. But human beings can be devilish. We may even say of someone, "He has the devil in him." If there is some truth in that observation, I would venture to say that one will find a devil in every narcissistic or psychopathic individual.

In any case, Mark and I discussed his reaction. I suggested that he didn't feel threatened because he had nothing to lose. His penis didn't belong to him anyway. This interpretation made sense to him. He then told me that he had always had the image that his body was a penis; his head was the glans while his body was the shaft. Could anything be more phallic or more narcissistic!

The image of the body as a phallus implies that Mark thought he had to be hard and strong. He prided himself on his erective potency, but while such potency is a precondition for orgasm, sexual pleasure and satisfaction depend on the discharge of the excitation and release of the tension. A man must surrender his erection to achieve orgasm. The emphasis on erective potency rather than orgastic potency stems from a commitment to be "there" for the woman. This was Mark's basic orientation in life. He had been seduced into this position by his mother's promise that he would be her "special" love. Unfortunately, as a child, Mark could not see the emptiness of this promise. He did become her "special" love, but at the expense of his sexuality and sexual feeling. He gave up his orgastic potency for an exaggerated erective potency, or, to put it another way, his personal fulfillment became secondary to that of his mother.

Mark's sacrifice didn't help his mother. He related that when he was ten, she began to drink heavily and use drugs. As a boy, then, he took it upon himself to watch over his mother and protect her from her self-destructive behavior. His father was less involved. Yet Mark's efforts were in vain, and he eventually turned against his mother for what he saw as a betrayal. Although this added a note of bitterness and anger to all his relations with women, it did not change his original position.

For women, Mark projected an image of a man able to produce (an erection) and able to maintain his (its) hardness and strength. He believed that this was what women wanted, and so it was a seductive ploy. Many women did respond, but the relationships never led to real satisfaction, for either partner. As I noted, Mark's two marriages had ended in divorce. Just as there was no deep satisfaction for Mark in his erective potency, there was none for the women either. Again, the sexual relationship between a man and woman is a very interdependent one. A man's climax will often trigger a woman's and vice versa. A woman may want her man to be hard and strong at times, but only if he can be soft and tender at others. Mark began to appreciate that his hardness was also a negative expression. It could be interpreted as saying: "You can't get to me. I won't feel anything."

Slowly, through our work, Mark's attitude and his body began to change. The expressed desire to be soft led to sobbing, which softened his body. His expression became different. When I first saw him, there was an angry, pained cast to his face. His brows were knitted in a distrustful, suspicious look. After crying deeply, his face brightened, his brows lifted, and his eyes cleared. He looked like a happy young boy. It seemed like the other side of the coin. The "face" of the hard, embittered, angry man had covered its exact opposite, in a reversal of the Dorian Gray theme.

Mark has always regarded himself as special and superior,

first in relation to his father and later in relation to other men. He was strong, he wasn't afraid of them, he could produce, and he could satisfy a woman—that was the image he projected and identified with. It gave him a sense of power in relation to women that was not greatly diminished by the failure of two marriages. As long as he could perform sexually (produce an erection), he was on top, he was successful. He used sex as a defense against feeling—his need for love, his fear of rejection, his orgastic impotence. Narcissists use sex as a substitute for love and intimacy.

Narcissists have a fear of intimacy because it requires an exposure of the self. One can't be intimate and hide behind a mask or image. But physical closeness makes no such demand and can be used to hide the self and feelings. Narcissists may use sexual closeness as a way to avoid true intimacy, for the darkness and the proximity are obstacles to seeing the other person. As a result, sex becomes a mechanical act between two bodies while the feelings are aroused by and focused on fantasy partners.

Awareness is a function of time and distance. Seeing another person takes time. If one is strongly focused on the pursuit of an objective, one only sees the other person as an image. One doesn't have time to make the change of focus necessary to allow the selfhood of the other to emerge clearly. To do so makes the other more important for the moment than one's goal, which is extremely difficult for narcissists. Distance or space is important for eye contact. If one carries someone on one's back, literally or figuratively speaking, one can't see nor be seen by him or her. Similarly, two people hugging can't see each other. Narcissists, being lonely people, go in for hugging, but I suspect that they do so because it is less threatening than seeing or being seen. However, hiding the self denies the self and ends in a loss of the self.

I counsel people to look before they touch. See who and

where the other person is before getting close, if a real feeling contact with the other is desired. The following incident illustrates the narcissism that passes as closeness. It occurred at a training workshop for therapists that I was conducting. My associate had just finished leading an exercise class and announced a period of unstructured body work. What he said was "Now you can do whatever you like." One woman exclaimed, "I want to give Al Lowen a big hug." With that she rushed at me like a mother at a lost child. Before she reached me, I put up my hand and said, "Stop. Why don't you find out first if I want to be hugged?" Obviously it hadn't occurred to her that I might have some feelings that should be considered. To submit without any feeling or desire on my part would be a denial of my selfhood. Acting impulsively as this woman did was a denial of her selfhood. After making her statement, which was genuine, she could have approached me, made eye contact, and said to me, "I would like to give you a hug." I am sure that if our eye contact was good, I would have responded warmly since she would have seen me as a person and not as the image she admired.

WHAT IS COMMON?

Do you recall the story of Jonathan Livingston Seagull? He was a "special" bird. He was not interested in screeching or squabbling with the other seagulls. He wanted no part of their fighting for a piece of rotten fish. He was above that. Where the other birds were content to remain within the limits of ordinary seagull life, Jonathan was obsessed with the idea of transcending those limits. So he went off on his own to become a pure spirit, interested only in pure love. No sex.

Does that choice make sense? Actually, as children,

narcissists didn't have a choice. They were seduced into giving up their sexuality and offered, in its place, the image of being special. It was a poor bargain, but they had no choice. They may even have thought that one day they would experience a special sexuality, transcending ordinary love. As adults, they may realize that that is only possible in their imagination. Yet having made the initial deal, they are reluctant to renounce it. After all, aren't they special? Why should they give that up? But if they don't give up the image of being special, they have no chance of recovering the sexuality that is common to all people.

In saying this, I'm not denying that people do have special gifts. We are each unique, with our own abilities and talents, which are different from those of other persons. But that does not make us "special," for we recognize that others also have special gifts and talents, which we may not possess. If we are wise, we don't base our identity on our special ability. Our special gifts are like the furnishings in our home. Without a house to contain them, to give them meaning, they are just pieces of furniture. In a house, they take on character and distinction reflecting the quality of life. Our body is our house. It is the foundation of our identity. Writing a book doesn't make me a man. Being a man, which is the essence of my nature, I can also be a writer. If one can identify with one's body as one's being, if one can say simply, "I am a man" or "I am a woman," one will discover that one's true identity derives from one's common heritage, not from one's specialness.

What do I mean by one's common heritage? How is one not special? What is common to all people is the body and its functioning. On a basic level, all bodies function similarly. To be special, one must deny one's identification with one's body, for that identification would mean that one is like everyone else. A patient described her narcissistic mother in these words: "She thinks her shit doesn't stink." And to be special, one must also deny one's feelings, for they, too, are common. Everyone loves, hates, and gets angry, sad, frightened, etc. The special person has to be above the body and its feelings.

Being special sets one apart. We refer to ordinary people as the common people. The common people have each other. They belong to the human race; they share the common struggle. But they are not tied to each other. The special person is bound initially to the individual who makes him or her feel special and later to those who regard him or her as special. The special person is not free—that is an illusion. Where the special person lives in the clouds, in images, the common people are grounded in the reality of life. They laugh and cry, have pleasure and pain, know sorrow and joy. They *live* their lives and so are fulfilled. The special person imagines a life. And in this way the special person does create a special destiny—to see his or her image crumble, as Dorian Gray did when reality confronted him.

As I have emphasized repeatedly, the true needs of a person are never satisfied through an image. A male is not fulfilled in his manhood by seducing women with a macho façade. No matter how effective his façade is, he will remain insecure inwardly as long as he is dependent on his façade. Because he cannot let go of it and give in to his feelings, his sexual responsiveness will suffer. Unfortunately, this lack of sexual fulfillment seems to confirm his inadequacy, leading him to invest more energy in the façade. His real need is to accept himself as he is, which means to accept all his feelings—his fears, anger, sadness, and even despair. In accepting himself, he will find his true maleness. The same considerations apply to the woman who tries to project an image of alluring femininity. The image does nothing to increase her sexual feelings and actually diminishes them, because energy or libido is withdrawn from body feeling and invested in the ego. True beauty, for both men and women, lies in an inner aliveness, not an external *show* of looks. I have often heard women exclaim at the end of a session in which they had released their sadness by deep crying, "I must look like a mess." In truth, their eyes were shining and their faces radiant. They looked beautiful.

6

Horror: The Face of Unreality

In Chapter 3, I pointed out how the denial of feeling that characterizes the narcissist differs from the absence of feeling in the catatonic schizophrenic. The catatonic's body goes rigid; nothing moves, and so there is nothing to feel. Not so with the narcissist. The narcissist moves about like an ordinary person. On the surface, it is difficult to detect the lack of feeling, except for two signs. One is the presence of a façade, which betrays the fact that the person is functioning in terms of an image rather than a feeling self. A façade is recognized by the fact that it always has a fixed expression; for example, the fixed smile that many people wear. A façade is really a mask which is characterized by its lack of aliveness. The other sign is a special look in the eyes—or, rather, the absence of a look. The eyes are dull; no light shines through them; there is no expression of feeling. This dullness of the eyes in no way reflects a dull mind. Quite the contrary. Mentally, narcissists are sharp and alert; their thinking is clear and logical. I have known narcissists who were tournament bridge players, computer experts, financial wizards, and shrewd lawyers. Their thinking, however, was not connected to feeling; their minds operated like computers. Eye contact is an expression of friendliness, for it represents a degree of intimacy that one doesn't accord to total strangers. It is interesting to note that the common form of greeting among some African natives is the expression "I see you."

It is true that one also sees an absence of feeling in the eyes of schizoid or schizophrenic individuals, but the quality is different. Schizophrenics' eyes have a faraway or vacant look, as if they were looking past you. While a part of them sees and hears you, another part is off somewhere else. When schizophrenics get this faraway look, we say their eyes go off. Narcissists' eyes never go off. Their minds don't depart from the reality of the situation they are in. Looking at you, they see you—but not as a feeling being, only as an image. It is as if they were seeing you as a reflection in a mirror. Thus, they can be aware of everything you do but still not see the essential you. In this sense, there is an important break with reality in the narcissist's personality, but it is not the same as the schizophrenic's break with reality. One would never call a narcissist crazy, however much a degree of insanity may be present in the depths of his or her personality (see Chapter 7). But why are the narcissist's eyes so dull?

I suggested earlier that narcissists cut off their feelings as a defense against vulnerability. Yet neurotics do the same. What, then, is unique to the narcissistic disorder? In my opinion, what makes for the difference is the experience of horror in the home situation. To understand the narcissistic disturbance, we have to know that people react to the experience of horror by denying the experience. We need to know exactly what "horror" is and what events in a home give rise to it. It was Paul who first made me conscious of the role of horror in the etiology of narcissism, so I shall begin with his case.

THE CASE OF PAUL

Paul, a man of about thirty-six, came to me with the primary complaint of depression. What surprised me in his case was my inability to evoke any emotional response in him. I noticed, however, that while doing some breathing exercises, Paul uttered sounds that made me think of old Jews at the

Wailing Wall in Jerusalem. When I pointed this out to him, Paul didn't react—he expressed neither interest nor surprise. His face was a mask.

One can penetrate such a mask by applying light pressure with the fingers to the cheekbones, alongside the nose. The pressure is on the risorius muscles and prevents the person from smiling. When I tried this maneuver with Paul, his face took on a very sad, lost look. His only comment, however, was: "I don't feel anything." I asked Paul to open his eyes wide while I continued the pressure. This exercise brought out a strong expression of fear. Yet, again, Paul's only comment was: "I don't feel anything."

Paul's physical appearance offered one clue to his problem. Although his body was well shaped, without any obvious distortions, I had the strong impression that his head was not connected to his body in an energetic sense. By this I mean that any movement or impulse that occurred in the body didn't extend to and involve the head. By the same token, Paul's perceptions and thoughts did not immediately influence his body's reactions. It is as if he were split—what went on in his body was not directly connected with what went on in his head. At the time I was working with Paul, I was only just becoming aware of how basic this kind of split is to narcissistic disturbances. I recall thinking that Paul lived predominantly in his head and how appropriate it was that he was a college professor.

Today I understand more clearly how the break in the connection between head and body is responsible for a person's lack of feeling. As I described in Chapter 3, the break is caused by a band of tension at the base of the skull, which blocks the subjective perception of bodily events. Whereas the person experiences thoughts subjectively as self-expressions, he or she experiences the body objectively—from without. Yet in contrast to the schizophrenic dissociation of head and body, in which the body is regarded as an alien object, the narcissist knows that it is his or her body. Paul was not schizoid or schizophrenic.

The dissociation of the head from the body in schizophrenic conditions is generally manifested by a lack of alignment between the axis of the head and that of the body. The head is tilted to one side, which may be so slight in some cases that only an experienced eye would detect it, or it may be quite evident depending on the degree of dissociation. In some cases, an exaggerated elongation of the neck reflects the separation. Neither of these signs is seen in the narcissistic disturbance, because the energetic connection between head and body has not been broken.

The theories I had evolved to explain those disorders were not applicable to Paul's case.[1] What had happened, then, to cause his disorder?

Paul was the youngest of three children, the two older ones being girls. As far as he could remember, his mother and father didn't get along. He related that his mother used to scream at his father and often became quite hysterical. His father, in turn, would fly into a violent rage, occasionally smashing some object and sometimes beating one of the girls. Paul looked on helplessly, unable to stop the parental madness. He himself did not recall ever being hit by his father. In describing all this, Paul spoke logically and coolly. He showed no emotion concerning the events he reported. It was as if they hadn't really happened to him. He could have been discussing a story he had read—a horror story, it is true, but one that didn't involve him. Or one might depict Paul's emotional detachment another way: In many respects, his childhood had a nightmarish quality. It was like a bad dream, which one dismisses as unreal when one is awake.

HORROR VERSUS TERROR

Before I worked with Paul, the concept of horror was not part of my analytic understanding of the emotional causes of illness. I did not include horror in the spectrum of emotions I presented and analyzed in my book *Pleasure*.[2] On the other hand, I had often referred to terror—a term often used interchangeably with horror—as an emotion, namely, as an extreme state of fear. The schizoid personality, for instance, develops as a reaction to terror, not horror. Unlike terror, however, horror is not an emotion, because there is no feeling quality to the state of horror.

According to the dictionary definition, "terror" denotes an intense fear, which is somewhat prolonged and may refer to imagined or future dangers. "Horror" implies a sense of shock and dread. The danger to which it refers contains an element of evil and may threaten others rather than the self. Although there may be an element of fear in horror (the Latin root of the word means "great fear"), it is not dominant. What predominates is a feeling of repulsion coupled with its opposite—attraction. Horror movies, foı example, build on this dual aspect.

Two characteristics of horror are important to our present discussion. One is the focus on a danger or harm to others. The other is the way the experience of horror affects the person. Imagine being faced with the prospect of an airplane crash yourself—it is terrifying. The idea of this accident happening to others, however, is horrifying. One is horrified at witnessing a brutal attack on another but terrified when the attack is against oneself. Soldiers may describe the terrors of war, but noncombatants tend to emphasize its horrors. Of course, war can be both terrifying and horrifying to those engaged in it. Understanding this, we can appreciate that

Paul's reaction to the violence in his home was one of horror.

Horror is not an emotion, because there is no movement or motion associated with it. In terror, on the other hand, there is an actual or potential motor force involved. Terror is related to the Greek word *trein* ("to flee") and to the Sanskrit word *trasati* ("he or she trembles"). Many of us have experienced the trembling or shaking that follows an escape from a dangerous accident; this is our reaction to terror at the prospect of serious injury. In horror, there is no physical reaction. According to the dictionary, the essence of horror is a "sense of shock," but I don't think that "shock" is the right word. Terror can produce a state of shock. When a cat digs its claws or teeth into a mouse, the mouse goes into a state of shock and doesn't feel the pain. We may observe that when the mouse is let go, temporarily, it lies still for a moment, paralyzed. If the shock passes, it attempts to escape. We say that a person is frozen with terror. In shock, blood is withdrawn from the surface of the body, paralyzing the voluntary musculature. As a result, the person becomes pale and often falls down in a faint. In the Florida Everglades, I once saw an alligator with a bird in its mouth. The bird was alive and conscious, but it was motionless. It did not struggle to get free. Of course, it couldn't escape, and a moment later the alligator submerged and drowned the bird. I am sure the bird felt no pain, because shock numbs the body. It acts as a local anesthetic.

In horror, in contrast to terror, the body is relatively unaffected, for there is no threat of physical danger. The effect of horror is primarily on the mind. Horror stuns the mind. It paralyzes the mental apparatus as terror paralyzes the physical apparatus. One may walk away from a scene of horror, seemingly unaffected physically, but one may be incapable of thinking about anything but the horror one has just witnessed. In one's mind, one goes over the scene again, and again, searching for some understanding. But one can find no explanation. One cannot integrate the experience, because horror is, by its very nature, incomprehensible. It lies in one's mind just as some indigestible food particle might lie in one's stomach, producing a similar sense of disgust and revulsion. One wants to throw it up to free oneself from it. This is the repulsive side of horror (I shall discuss its attraction later).

Dracula and Frankenstein's monster are typical of horror movie characters. Dracula, risen from the dead and drinking the blood of innocent victims, is a fantasy image. But in some sense he must be real because of the effect this image has on us. The idea that some creature would drink human blood may be fantasy today, but it could have been a real phenomenon in man's early evolutionary history when he was vulnerable to animal predators. If we pictured such an attack upon ourselves, we would be filled with terror. In a horror movie, the terror is minimum since we feel relatively safe; it fascinates and repels us, and we react to the horror only.

But this effect may also have something to do with the fact that in early times mankind pictured the world as full of good and bad spirits, benevolent gods and goddesses opposing monsters and demons. Greek mythology is replete with stories of heroes fighting with monsters, like Hercules' destruction of Hydra—a nine-headed serpent with breath so poisonous that whoever it touched fell dead—or Perseus' destruction of Medusa—one of the Gorgon sisters, who was so horrifying that whoever looked her in the face instantly turned to stone. These monsters represent the wild, uncontrollable, and incomprehensible forces of nature. Human victory over these horrors symbolize man's ability to overcome this primitive fear of the unknown through courage, strength, and intelligence. For most people today, nature—even at its most frightening (hurricanes or earthquakes)—does not present itself as monstrous or nightmarish. However, the victory is not fully won; there are still incomprehensible forces in human nature that can evoke a sense of horror in us. Dracula and Frankenstein's monster are human-like monsters.

Unfortunately, there are human monsters, too. Hitler, for example, was seen as a monster by many people, and pictures of the Nazi concentration camps still evoke a sense of horror in us. Human monsters are characterized by their lack of human feelings. Mass murderers, sex criminals, and muggers are regarded as monsters. Their behavior is incomprehensible to a normal person and evokes a sense of horror. An all-too-common example is the following: A mother walking with her six-year-old son on the streets of New York City was mugged and brutally beaten. The little boy looked on in horror, but he seemed untouched. His mind, as I imagine it, could only think, "No. It's impossible. It shouldn't be happening. Why? I don't understand it." He saw the muggers as monsters.

Horror is not the only reaction to an incomprehensible event. Awe is another possible reaction. A situation that cannot be taken in (comprehended) by the mind will be viewed with horror or awe, depending on whether it has negative or positive connotations for the viewer. Seeing an armada of planes fly overhead to bomb the enemy can be awesome. The same armada, seen by the enemy, may evoke a feeling of terror if one believes oneself to be personally threatened by the attack, or horror if the attack seems directed elsewhere and one feels safe. However, in most situations of horror, there is some element of terror, since one cannot avoid some identification with the victim, and so one does experience some degree of fear.

The distinction between horror and terror enables us to understand an essential difference between the narcissistic and schizoid disturbances. The schizoid personality stems directly from the experience of terror. (My book *The Betrayal of the Body* makes this clear.) The schizoid body is frozen—frozen with terror. It is in a state of shock; blood and energy are withdrawn from the surface of the body, often leaving it cold and unalive. The body of the narcissistic individual is relatively unaffected by the experience of horror. The inability to respond emotionally stems from the denial of feelings that are potentially present in the body. But the experiences of horror and terror are not mutually exclusive. A person can be subject to both with the result that his or her personality may show both schizoid and narcissistic tendencies. The evaluation of such a case depends on the degree of each factor. It becomes a matter of clinical judgment.

HORROR IN THE FAMILY

We can return now to Paul's case and comprehend how living with a hysterical mother and violent father was a nightmare for him. Their behavior was incomprehensible, especially because he believed that his parents cared for each other and their children. As with any nightmare, Paul tried to forget what he had seen. But one cannot easily forget a nightmare—all one can do is to pass it off as belonging to another world, an unreal world. One dissociates it. This is what Paul did. He dissociated himself from his past by denying its reality. He cut off any feeling of longing to be close to either parent, which enabled him to deny his sadness, anger, and fear. The block against feeling was so effective it was almost impossible to evoke any feeling in the therapy. Life, however, took a hand in this situation. Paul's father developed cancer, and the family, faced with this tragedy, allowed their caring and concern for each other to show. Before Paul could cry about his own pain, he cried for the pain and tragedy of his father's illness.

Paul's reaction to the horror of his childhood was not unusual. In a situation of horror, all of us have a tendency to disbelieve our senses because they contradict our image of reality. To question our sense of reality would make us feel disoriented and crazy. Instead, to protect our sanity, we dissociate the experience—it becomes unreal, a bad dream. How does it lead to a narcissistic disturbance? If the experience of horror is a solitary one, the dissociation is limited to that situation. But if, as in Paul's case, the horror is continuous, if one *lives* in such a situation, the dissociation becomes structured in one's body as a split between the perceptual functions of the mind and the sensing functions of the body. Denying one's emotions becomes a habit, engraved in the personality. Action is taken solely on the basis of reason and logic. One lives in a world divorced from feeling. Indeed, the world of feeling is seen as unreal and, therefore, allied to insanity. Although such a person knows about feelings, he or she cannot let go to feelings—that is, allow them to "dictate" behavior. Even when Paul talked about the horror of the Holocaust, his words were not connected to any feeling. He was still too caught up in the sense of horror about what happened to his family and to Jews in general to be able to speak with feeling about these events. The only way to overcome the effect of horror on the personality is to activate the person's feelings so he or she can abreact these painful experiences—cry about them, get angry, or both. We saw earlier that when Paul did a breathing exercise designed to activate feeling, he made wailing sounds suggesting pain and sorrow, but he did not identify with them. He denied their meaning.

People who have lived through experiences of horror in their childhood have an unreal quality in their personalities. They can describe a past that makes the listener shudder, yet they themselves speak in a calm, phlegmatic voice. Not only do they seem out of touch with the feeling self, but they seem equally out of touch with the listener as a feeling person. Their eyes see you but don't touch you. A shell has covered over the experience of horror. That experience lies buried—a time bomb whose explosion might produce insanity.

How common is the childhood experience of horror? In terms of screaming and fighting parents, I would say it is fairly common. In Chapter 3, I presented the case of Linda, who had denied all feeling. As a child, she used to bury her head under the covers so as not to hear her parents yelling at each other. She said she couldn't stand it. A recent story in the *New York Post* reported the attempted suicide of two young boys, who claimed they couldn't stand their parents' constant fighting and shouting. Most children learn to stand their parents' fighting, but the price they pay is a dissociation from the world of feeling.

Fighting isn't the only form of horror in a family, as the case of Burt, a narcissistic personality with psychopathic tendencies, indicated. Burt described his mother as a religious fanatic. Whenever he became ill or distressed, she responded with the assurance that if only he believed in Christ, everything would be all right. Such an attitude may be helpful to an adult, who is capable of placing faith in a nonmaterial entity, but it is incomprehensible to a child, whose faith is in the parents. And it wasn't only her religious fervor that made Burt's mother into a monster in his eyes. She was hard and insensitive, with an almost complete lack of human feeling and empathy. Yet she managed to seduce Burt into a "special" relationship with her, thus alienating the boy from his father and depriving him of any warmth and support from that source. Living under her control and domination was a nightmare for Burt, which resulted in his cutting off all feeling. His big complaint was that life had no meaning for him.

I heard a somewhat similar story from another patient—Charles—who was a psychologist. His father had left the family when Charles was three years old. His mother then became a religious fanatic, and completely ignored Charles. Despite the fact that he had older brothers, Charles felt himself to be a stranger in his home. He became afraid of his mother whom he saw as cold and insensitive and, thus, passed many years growing up in a state of lonely desperation. When I saw him as a young man, he had a beatific expression on his face but no trace of feeling. I pictured Charles as a medieval monk, living alone and withdrawn from a day-to-day world that made no sense. In reality, his underlying hostility against his mother prevented him from following in her religious footsteps. But to be in the world, he had to make some sense of it, and he tried to do this by becoming a psychologist.

Psychology as the study of human behavior attempts to make sense of actions that run counter to natural tendencies. One doesn't need psychology to explain why a child drinks a glass of water. That makes sense because it quenches thirst. But when a child acts self-destructively—refusing to eat, for instance—we will call on psychology to explain such unnatural behavior. Similarly, we don't need psychology to explain a mother's love for her child. But we do need psychology to explain a mother's destructive behavior toward her child. The same holds for a father. And it doesn't make sense to children if their parents do not behave lovingly toward each other. How can one expect a child to comprehend his or her parent's hostility toward each other? The child would have to be a psychologist.

Sense and sanity go together. Actions don't always have to make sense. There is room in our minds for nonsense. But with nonsense, we know that it isn't intended to make sense, so it doesn't disturb our sense of reality. When things that are supposed to make sense don't, it feels like craziness. When parents behave in an unloving way, the child feels that the situation is crazy. It doesn't make sense. But can a child say to his or her mother, "Look, you're acting crazy; you're supposed to love me"? If the child did, the mother might answer, "I do love you, but you are a bad child." Good and bad are sophisticated concepts, which the child learns only slowly. The child's immediate reaction is to think, "There must be something wrong with me. I am crazy because I expect my mother to love me regardless of what I do." Since mother stands as the final arbiter of reality, the child must accept the mother's position as sensible and sane. The child's natural feelings of longing and love are then seen as crazy.

The Case of Laura

It was the dullness in Laura's eyes that made me constantly aware of the horror in her childhood. Laura could be described as a borderline personality, for her sense of self was extremely deficient. Her body was undercharged, without much energy. Her skin was cold and damp, her breathing shallow, her musculature underdeveloped. Surprisingly, even though she ran five miles every day, her legs looked weak, thin, and underdeveloped. And her voice seemed even weaker. Laura might have enough will for her running, but she didn't have enough to communicate with me. Specifically, she couldn't get her voice out whenever she had any feeling. Her voice simply failed if she wanted to protest "no" or if she tried to make a loud, angry roar. Nor could Laura cry; no sounds broke through her constricted throat. Obviously, in the first phase of her therapy, I worked on helping her to breathe more deeply and to mobilize her voice. Eventually, Laura did let out a scream and a cry, significantly improving her condition.

Laura developed a strong transference to me. Often I found her looking at me as she lay on the bed after some exercise, her eyes fixed on my face. On one occasion, as she gazed at me, I studied her eyes carefully. They were wide open, with the pupils fully dilated, despite the fact that the room was brightly lit. They had a dull, staring quality—the look of horror. Intrigued by this, I asked Laura what she saw. "I love to look at your face," she mused. "You have the gentlest face."

Laura's statement so contradicted the horror in her eyes that I wondered if she might be thinking of someone else while looking at me. "Yes," she responded, "my father." Realizing that her eyes reflected her experience of her father, I asked Laura to tell me about him.

"He was a very handsome man—tall, an actor," Laura recounted. "But I saw in his eyes that he wanted to kill me."

"Why?" I interjected.

"We were living in one room in a hotel," Laura explained. "He wanted my mother, and I was in the way. He used to say to me, 'Go take a walk, kid.' When he was angry, his face became ugly, distorted. I couldn't believe that my daddy could turn into a monster. I recall as a little girl sitting on his shoulders and his holding me. It felt so good."

Her mother and father had separated when Laura was three. Her mother told her that it was because of her. Laura's father went to Hollywood to work as an actor, but he returned when Laura was about nine or ten. He had not succeeded.

Laura continued her story: "He looked so bad. He had had all his teeth capped in order to be an actor, but he was in an automobile accident and all the caps were knocked loose. He had all his lower teeth pulled out. He used to lie in bed and scream. It was awful. I couldn't stand it. I would run out of the house. I couldn't stand his pain."

During her father's absence, Laura and her mother had moved about from place to place. She described their relationship as symbiotic: "I felt my mother and I were one person. She was at me all the time. So when my father came back, I turned to him. But it was a horrible mistake because when he hurt me, I couldn't complain. I couldn't tell anyone. He used to hit me when he was frustrated or angry. Once he knocked me against the wall. But I didn't cry. I felt so sorry for him. He was such a tragic figure."

Laura's feelings toward her father were ambivalent. On another occasion, she depicted him as "dark, brooding, stormy." He frightened her, but she also felt that he was like a little boy whom she had to protect. She would have done anything to make him happy. "But," she admitted, "he was like a greedy infant. Everything had to be for him, and he became obnoxious. I fulfilled his narcissistic needs. He needed to be admired, and I admired him. He never really knew me. Then I grew to hate him, which made me hate myself."

One aspect of the horror in Laura's situation was that it didn't make sense. Her father treated her viciously, yet he also did things that made her aware of his love for her. She related that her father gave blood to get the money to buy her a gift. I would guess that she also, on occasion, glimpsed softness or tenderness in his eyes, which touched her deeply. But sustaining such an openness was beyond her father. It made him feel too vulnerable, so he cut it off. The tragedy of narcissists is that on some deep level, they desperately want to love and be loved, but they cannot or dare not express these feelings. It would evoke too much pain.

Laura's problem was the reverse of her father's. His grandiosity dovetailed with her insignificance; his need to be admired met her need to admire. The disturbance, however, was the same—an inability to love. Both had loved; both had been seduced and betrayed. Her father had been seduced by his mother into thinking himself special. And on some level, Laura also saw herself as special—she devoted herself to making others happy. But such self-sacrifice is no substitute for love.

Beneath the betrayal and the hurt in narcissistic characters and borderline personalities is the original love. That love is the only thing that can give the person a valid sense of self, a sense of a lovable self and one capable of loving. Laura had transferred to me both the admiration and love she had for her father. Could she express that love and her longing? As she lay on the bed, I asked her to reach up with her arms, like a child, and say, "Daddy, daddy." No sound came out. Her throat contracted, and a look of intense pain flashed over her face. It was too much. She couldn't let herself sense the depth of her longing or the extent of her pain.

As I noted earlier, Laura had already made considerable progress in her therapy, opening herself more and more to me. I could get her to scream by applying some pressure to the tight muscles on the sides of her neck. Hers was never a full-throated scream, but often it ended in some sobbing. She also kicked the bed, protesting "Why?" or "No." But both the sounds and the movements lacked force and conviction. Most times she had to mobilize her will to start the exercise. Still, every expression of feeling was difficult for her. It was hard for her to voice her feelings toward me, whether loving or angry. And she had not yet been able to truly express, not just describe, her feelings toward her parents. But only by expressing feeling can a person gain contact with the true self. It is slow work, for both the physical defenses (the muscular tensions) and the psychological defenses (the denial) must be reduced.

What was the danger Laura feared? What would happen if she voiced her feelings? In Laura's mind, if she let herself go fully, allowing her feelings their voice, she would emerge a shrieking maniac. She envisioned herself going crazy. I didn't see it that way. Laura might scream like a maniac, but her screaming would be appropriate to the horror of her childhood situation. It would make sense. Yet however much I might be able to explain her denial of feeling psychologically, it didn't make sense. Denying one's feelings is crazy because it is a denial of the self. The narcissism of Laura's father had more than a touch of insanity in it. And a parent's insanity, expressed in the denial of feeling, both terrifies and horrifies a child.

It would be an error, however, to regard Laura's relationship with her father as the sole cause of her problem. She herself described the distorted, symbiotic tie to her mother. Laura's mother used her—asking Laura to be "there" for her (the mother). At the same time, Laura was deprived of the nurturing she herself needed to fill out her own being. The thinness and weakness of Laura's body, the tightness in her jaw and throat, her feeling of inner emptiness—all suggested a severe degree of oral deprivation. For a mother to demand that an undernurtured child respond to the mother's needs is another form of craziness. And whatever its form, craziness produces a sense of horror.

In my opinion, the underlying insanity of a narcissistic parent is more difficult for a child to handle than a parent's outright nervous breakdown. Of course, dealing with a breakdown is not easy, but in that situation the child knows who is crazy. With the narcissistic parent, the façade of sanity confuses the child. As a child, how can one be sure of oneself, one's feelings, and one's sensing in the face of a parent's arrogance and seeming certainty? What choice is there but to conform to the parent's sense of reality? Often it comes as a shock to a patient when I suggest that his or her parents' behavior showed some degree of craziness. At first, most patients tend to deny the idea of parental insanity, perhaps because it might raise questions in their minds about their own sanity. Some patients, however, are aware of the craziness in their families.

The Case of Ron

Ron, a highly successful young man, consulted me because of sexual impotence. He recognized that his impotence was related to an overall lack of feeling. Moreover, he connected this to the madness in his early home life. In his words: "There was a lot of craziness in my family. The way I survived was by turning it off.

"My mother never stopped talking," Ron went on to explain. "She would remind me all the time how hard she worked. She was like a TV set always turned on. I would shut myself in my room. Then my father would bang on my door because I upset her. I didn't respect him. He was a weak man. Stingy. It was very important for him that I be successful.

"The craziness," Ron reflected, "was all the movement. Three children competing for attention, talking. My mother constantly talking. My father putting her down. Each person acting a role. Fighting and yelling. It was chaotic. There was no sense, no philosophy, no meaning, no structure, and no plan to their lives."

And Ron was also aware of how his mother had tried to seduce him. "I was the receptacle of her affection," he recalled. "She brought cupcakes to school for me. But she also resented me and hit me."

Ron kept his sanity by cutting off his feelings. Another brother was less fortunate; he became a schizophrenic. Still, Ron paid a price for his sanity—the loss of his aliveness, his feelings. He had escaped the craziness of his family by locking himself up in his own body, where no one could reach him. But as an adult, he discovered that he couldn't come out—he was locked in tight. His body had become a machine—steady, hard, and efficient but incapable of any spontaneous movement. For Ron to let go of his rigidity and control posed a risk—his defense against insanity might collapse. It wouldn't, but Ron couldn't be sure. On one occasion in therapy, his anger broke forth, after which he enjoyed a spell of well-being, with sexual feeling. Although this didn't last, it increased his incentive to break out of his shell and experience life.

PATTERNS OF CHILD REARING

Adults often fail to appreciate the horrors and terrors that pervade the lives of so many children. Even if they have experienced some of these horrors themselves, they, like Ron, may have switched off any emotional resonance. In conversations about the different patterns of child rearing, they logically and coolly measure the advantages and disadvantages to parents but ignore the impact on the child. Recently, I was at a party, which was attended by a young couple expecting their first child. A discussion arose about whether a mother should stay home with her child or return to work as soon as possible. The issue did not revolve about the couple's financial need but on the question of the mother's career. The prospective mother was undecided about her choice. She held an important position in the business world. Many of her friends had gone back to work soon after the birth of their babies. One woman, for instance, was a busy executive during the day and a frantic mother at night, who screamed at her child. The discussion then focused on how difficult it was for a woman to have patience with a child after a day of pressure in the office. But no one expressed sympathy for a child who is constantly exposed to a distraught mother. And no one was disturbed by a style of life in which the interest of the mother might conflict with that of her child. In my opinion, that is a big horror.

We must remember that what is horrifying to a child

may not be horrifying to an adult, whose sophisticated mind has a broader grasp of reality. An example that comes to mind is the operating room in a hospital. In all probability, a young child witnessing an operation would be horrified by the scene, seeing masked people standing around a table and calmly cutting open the body of the helpless person lying on it. How can a child conceive that the person feels no pain or comprehend the lifesaving potential of the procedure? In contrast, an adult observer might feel a sense of awe at the technical achievement that a major operation represents. To witness such a scene without a sense of horror or awe would require, it seems to me, a total negation of feeling. As a medical intern assisting at some operations, I found it hard to be detached and indifferent to the situation, even though I could comprehend the procedure and its necessity. And when I assisted at deliveries and watched an obstetrician pull a baby out of the mother's body with forceps, I experienced horror. Although this procedure was almost routine in the hospital where I interned, I could not comprehend its necessity, for I had also assisted at deliveries in which every effort was made to avoid trauma or insult to the mother or baby. Watching a natural birth, with the mother conscious, is awe inspiring. Ideally, I would like to see babies born at home, which is a more natural environment than a hospital. A home delivery, I think, would provide both parents with a better sense of the reality of parenthood than a hospital delivery.

The next natural step is breast-feeding the child. There is something that seems so right about a mother breast-feeding a child. Mouth and teat are so obviously made for each other; the fit is so perfect. This concept of fitness and rightness is basic to our sense of reality. Watching a bird fly or a fish swim makes sense to us. I believe that we and other organisms are born with a sense of the rightness of things, stemming from the evolutionary history of the species. A baby bird emerging from its shell carries the expectation in its body that a mother bird will be there to feed it, warm it, and protect it. That is what the reality of bird life is. Similarly, a human newborn has the biological expectation that a human mother will be available in the way that human mothers have been for countless aeons.*

Thus, infants expect a teat to be available for their nourishment; they are programmed to suck a teat from the moment of birth. That expectation may be fulfilled in part by a bottle with a rubber nipple. Yet the impulse to suck, and seemingly the need, is so strong that bottle-fed babies will often supplement the bottle by sucking on their thumbs. I have not seen any breast-fed babies do this if the breast-feeding was carried on long enough. Sucking provides a sense of security to the baby, but it also promotes better breathing.

Another biological expectation in the newborn is being close to the mother's body. The importance of this physical contact has been clearly demonstrated by Harry Harlow in his now-famous experiments with monkeys.[4] Harlow showed that infant monkeys deprived of this contact failed to develop normally and were psychologically disturbed. For human infants, lack of physical closeness to a mother or mother-substitute has similar effects, according to several studies. The babies become depressed and lose the ability to respond emotionally to people.[5]

Deprivation seems to affect the emotional development of a child in much the same way that horror does. Do the two situations, then, have something in common? To my mind, both conflict with the individual's inborn sense of the natural order of things. Both contain an element of unreality, making them incomprehensible to the individual. No infant or child can fathom the lack of response to his or her needs by a

* This concept of biological expectations deriving from the evolutionary history of a species is ably set forth by Jean Liedloff in *The Continuum Concept*.[3]

mother or father. The child's sense of reality is upset. Such a child must feel like a fish out of water as he or she cries and struggles to reestablish the expected environment. If the deprivation is not life threatening, the child will adjust. The deprivation is accepted as the new reality, but only after the child has waged and lost the battle for a human right.

One of the ways children are made to adjust to the new order is called "letting them cry themselves out." The mother puts the child into the crib at night to sleep. It is bedtime. But the sense of aloneness and the loss of contact with the mother's body terrifies the child, who begins to scream and cry. No animal mother would fail to respond to a baby's cry. Some human mothers believe, however, that to respond would be wrong. To give in to a child's crying will spoil the child. Besides, they have been told, crying is good for a child. It strengthens the lungs. So no response is made, and the child continues to cry.

The first time this happens, the child may cry for hours before falling asleep, exhausted. If the same procedure is repeated the next night, the child will not cry so long before falling asleep. The mother may think the child has learned a lesson, but, quite simply, the child doesn't have the energy for a repeat performance. Sleep comes more easily because exhaustion sets in more quickly. After several experiences of this kind, the child learns to give up the struggle for contact with the mother. In effect, the child has cut off the longing for this contact and so no longer feels the pain of frustration. A new reality, in which the desire for intimacy and closeness is not expressed, has been accepted. The foundations for narcissism and the borderline personality have been laid.

Parents may also react violently to a baby's crying. I have seen a parent hit a child to stop the crying. Threats of abandonment or punishment are commonly employed. In most cases of child abuse, the violence against the child is triggered by crying. Isn't that insane? It's like heaping fuel on a fire to stop it from burning. Yet some parents seem to be driven wild by a child's crying. They can't stand it, because it evokes their own suppressed crying, and they will hit their children as they were hit when they were young. Such situations combine terror and horror for the child. The horror may come out in nightmares which seem "silly" to their parents. In the children's eyes, the parents have become monsters. As adults, we may fail to see this monstrosity because, like the adults in the tale of the emperor's new clothes, we have been seduced or threatened into denying the truth.

The Case of Margaret

I commented earlier on the horror for children of parents who yell and fight with each other. There is an equal horror in homes in which all feelings are denied and given the gloss of "we are a happy family," as came out in my work with a young woman recently.

Margaret complained of a lack of sexual feeling. Her pelvis felt as if a steel band were encircling it. Since it is necessary to understand the origin of a tension before one can release it, I asked Margaret to describe her early life. "I have only happy memories of my childhood," she told me. "My mother and father never quarreled. They were very quiet and never raised their voices in anger. Feelings simply were not expressed." Margaret admitted that in this climate it was difficult for her to express anger, or even to cry. There was never any mention of sex in the family. The parental attitude was uprightly religious, but there was no preaching against sex. How can we explain Margaret's radical cutoff of sexual feeling?

Margaret informed me that there had been a period in her life when she was quite free sexually and orgastic. That was after the breakup of her first marriage. For more than a year, she was sexually promiscuous and completely uninhibited in her sexual activity. She claimed that she enjoyed multiple orgasms. Then she met the man who became her second husband. Initially, sex with him was exciting, but when the relationship deepened and they got married, her sexual feelings diminished, then disappeared. This lack of sexual feeling had also characterized her relationship with her first husband.

Margaret's appearance struck me as that of a prim, prudish schoolteacher. The large glasses on her small, round but expressionless face supported this impression. And it accorded with her lack of sexual feeling. Yet Margaret knew there was another side to her personality, behind the puritanical façade.

I saw Margaret as having a double personality rather than the split personality that characterizes the schizoid or schizophrenic state. In the split personality, the two aspects are present at the same time, whereas in the double personality, only one or the other can be seen at a time. Had Margaret been schizoid, her straitlaced appearance would have been belied by reckless, wanton behavior. One would always have been aware of the split. But Margaret could be only one or the other. As a prim, proper married woman, she had no sexual feelings. When she shed this role or stepped out from behind her façade, she was a different person. Seeing one aspect, one had difficulty imagining the other. It was a Dr. Jekyll–Mr. Hyde combination.

The personality of a child is shaped by the parents' personalities. As a married woman, Margaret identified with her mother, who presented the same prudish appearance. But what about her father? When I asked her about him—what work he did, for example—I was startled by her answer. "He's a safecracker," she said. I envisioned another double personality, but Margaret's father wasn't a criminal. His work entailed installing and maintaining safes. But from

Margaret's remark about safecracking, I pictured the steel band around her pelvis as a kind of chastity belt, which she wore while married but discarded when she was free. The pelvic tension kept her "safe"—safe for her husband. It did this by cutting off sexual desire and thus preventing the acting out of sexual impulses. But it was not the husband who was responsible for the psychological chastity belt. Such muscular tension develops in childhood, as a result of the Oedipal situation.

Why did Margaret call her father a safecracker, not a safe installer? Considered as a Freudian slip, her remark suggests that he and he alone could crack the safe, that he had the key to her true sexuality. On one level of her personality, Margaret belonged to her father. She could love another man, but if she did, she could not have any sexual feelings for him. She could have sex with other men, but she could not love them. Only with her father was her love and her sexuality combined. But that was before she put on the chastity belt, before she became guilty about the incestuous nature of her relationship to her father. When that guilt developed, she cut off her sexual feelings for her father, retaining on a conscious level only her love for him. Because the men she married took the place of her father in her affection, she couldn't allow any sexual feeling for them to surface.

At the beginning of her therapy, Margaret was completely unaware that there was a sexual element in her relationship with her father. She denied ever having any sexual feelings for him, although she was knowledgeable enough to recognize that such feelings would have been normal. Paradoxically, it was talking about her relationship to her mother that brought an awareness of these sexual feelings into being.

The discussion began at a workshop in which Margaret participated. In presenting her problems to this group of therapists, I remarked that Margaret was somewhat out of contact with herself. One of the participants commented that

Margaret looked as if she were in a state of shock. Margaret countered that she didn't feel that was true. I agreed with Margaret and suggested that her condition was more one of being stunned than shocked. Yes, she replied, that felt right to her.

What was the horror in her childhood that stunned her? I could only guess at this point that it was an atmosphere of unreality in her family. When I remarked that her family was anything but a happy one, Margaret recalled that her mother had insisted on everyone smiling and looking happy no matter what was happening. Then Margaret showed me how her mother had smiled—it was gargoylish. Her mouth opened wide, but the upper part of her face remained frozen. But this was Margaret's expression, too, when she tried to smile. It became obvious to me, then, that Margaret identified with her mother and that both were very unhappy people. Their attempt to cover their pain with a happy face made them appear unreal, gargoylish. For a child, the horror that resides in the denial of feeling is quite evident. As a child, Margaret had seen her mother's pain despite her mother's efforts to deny it. She was bewildered by a maneuver that made no sense.

Once Margaret admitted her mother's unhappiness, it became possible to uncover the real situation between her parents. Their amiability was a pretense. There was little affection and little sex between them. Margaret then realized that her father had focused much of his sexual feeling on her while denying any overt sexual interest in her. She was caught in a bind. Her father's interest excited her sexually, but she was also pained by her mother's displeasure at this. Because sexuality was not openly accepted by her parents, she felt very guilty about her feelings. She saw herself as responsible for the situation and reacted by cutting off any sexual feelings for her father. Thus, she became a "good" girl, her parents' child, playing their game of denying reality.

To break the grip of this denial on Margaret's personality, it was necessary to confront her with a reality that could snap her back into true sanity. That reality was the effect her face could have on her own child. I imitated her smile so she could see its gargoyle quality. Then, I had her look in a mirror to see how it looked on her own face. She was shocked at how monstrous she looked and recognized the horror for a child. She then realized that she was unconsciously doing to her child the same thing her mother had done to her. This understanding opened the door to her feelings and enabled her slowly to work through her narcissistic problem.

Throughout this book, I have suggested that there is some relationship between narcissism and insanity. We have seen that there is some degree of unreality in narcissists which might make one question their sanity. Up to this point, I have explained the narcissistic denial of feelings largely on the basis that they were unacceptable, contradicting, as they did, the projected image. There is, I believe, a more important reason for the denial of feelings, and that is the fear of insanity should they erupt and overwhelm the ego.

7

The Fear of Insanity

IS THERE a potential for insanity in all narcissists? We have just seen in the preceding chapter that the experience of horror makes one question one's sanity. What one is experiencing doesn't make sense, it doesn't accord with one's image of reality which even a baby has on a biological level. To avoid the resulting mental confusion, one must dissociate and deny all feelings connected with the experience. That is, one must cut off all feeling. As long as one sticks to logic, one is safe. But feelings are life, and one cannot fully avoid emotional experiences no matter how coolly one plays it. The narcissist faces the risk of being overwhelmed by feelings and going wild, crazy, or mad, should his defense of denial break down. This is especially true of anger. Every narcissist is afraid of going crazy, because the potential for insanity is in his personality. This fear reinforces the denial of feeling, creating a vicious circle.

THE CASE OF BILL

Bill, a middle-aged psychiatrist, consulted me about a low-grade depression, which he had had for many years despite intensive therapy. His body was heavy, without much life, and his face had a defeated expression, which was largely due to a retracted jaw that hung loosely. In his eyes I detected a mixture of sadness and fear. Bill, however, claimed that although he had experienced some sadness, he had never felt afraid. That seemed so unusual that I suspected he was denying his fear.

I asked Bill if he had ever been in a frightening situation. Yes, he recollected an incident some years ago that could have been frightening. He was riding in a car with a friend, also a psychiatrist, along a town street, and they stopped to pick up a hitchhiker. The man looked a little weird, but being psychiatrists, they felt they could handle any situation. About a mile from town, the hitchhiker, who was riding in the back seat, took out a rock he was carrying and struck Bill and his friend on their heads. Bill reported that he collapsed, thinking, "I'm a goner. He will kill me." His friend, who was driving, stopped the car, whereupon the hitchhiker muttered, "I'm sorry. I'm sorry," and made no effort to continue the attack or to escape. Eventually he was taken away by the police. By then, it was obvious that he was crazy. Bill and his friend were taken to a hospital for their head wounds, which required many stitches. "But," Bill assured me, "I felt no fear."

Because, normally, such a situation would call for fear, it can be assumed that Bill was denying or blocking the feeling—unconsciously, of course. I tried another tack. Most boys have some fear of their fathers because of the Oedipal conflict, so I asked Bill about his relationship with his father. He described his father as a strong, violent man who used to hit him. "How did he hit you?" I inquired. "Did he spank you?" "No," Bill answered, "he used to hit me on the head with his fists." "What did you do?" I then asked. "I tried to protect my head with my arms," Bill explained, "but he would continue to hit me until I fell to the floor." Although Bill's father was not psychotic, his behavior toward his son was insane on some level. How strange that Bill had experienced a similar attack from a crazy person in adulthood!

Equally strange, however, was Bill's complete incapacity to fight back. Once he was struck, he collapsed into a state of helplessness. Even now, as he related these stories, Bill did not feel any anger. He denied his anger just as he denied his fear. Instead, he adopted an attitude of submission and attempted to understand the irrational behavior of his father and others. His submission to his father may have had a lifesaving value, but it almost cost him his life in the later incident.

Bill was not a weak man physically. He had large hands and a muscular body. As a boy, he was no match for his father, but as he grew older and stronger, he probably could have beaten his father in a fight. Many men have told me how, in their late teens, they stopped their fathers' violence by standing up to them. That idea, however, was alien to Bill, though he conceded that it would have been possible. Bill's inability to fight back or resist might be explained by saying that he was terrified (even if he denied this). And in view of the beatings he took from his father, one has to assume that there was enough rage in Bill to kill. A murderous rage seems to be present in every person who was beaten as a child. Yet as an adult, Bill kept that rage suppressed, because to express it would mean that he was as crazy as his "mad" father. To protect his sanity, Bill had to disclaim his rage. He was determined not to go mad (be angry).

Bill believed that if he lost his head he might kill someone. But to lose your head is equivalent to going crazy. Bill was terrified of the potential craziness in himself as he was of the craziness in others. When I made this interpretation to him, he remarked, "Now I know why I became a psychiatrist."

My interpretation was not pure conjecture, for I could feel the tension in the muscles at the base of Bill's skull, where he held on to his head. Bill, too, was aware of this tension. To test my hypothesis, I proposed to Bill that I give a light karate chop to the base of his skull while his head was bent. He agreed, but when I raised my hand, he looked up at me and said, "I'm afraid." It was the first time he had admitted this feeling, and this represented a breakthrough.

THE EXPLOSION OF THE PSYCHOPATH

Bill was in touch with his potential craziness and afraid of it. He held on to his head because he sensed he could kill. But other narcissists, whose egos are weaker, are unable to contain their murderous rage. What is a potential for insanity in Bill becomes an act of insanity in the psychopathic killer.

David Berkowitz, also known as "Son of Sam," killed six persons and wounded seven others, none of whom he knew personally. When he was finally caught and arrested, he blamed his actions on demons who, he contended, ordered him to commit the murders. The question of his sanity hinged on whether the voices were psychotic hallucinations or whether he invented them to avoid responsibility for his actions. Two different psychiatrists declared him insane. Yet the psychiatrist for the prosecution and the judge decided Berkowitz was sane. Obviously, a court cannot take the position that a defendant is both sane and insane. But that is often the case.

David Abrahamsen, the psychiatrist for the prosecution, asserted: "Berkowitz showed himself to be alert, perceptive, and highly intelligent."[1] People who knew him described him as "like any other person." He was said to be courteous and helpful to female co-workers and was regarded as a "good and reliable employee." Yet there is the fact that he stalked and killed a number of women, which is hardly the behavior of a sane person. Evidently, Berkowitz had a split personality or what might be called, more properly, a double personality. One personality acted and behaved like any other person, the other was a monster, in Dr. Jekyll–Mr. Hyde fashion.

Abrahamsen concluded that Berkowitz "had a character disorder with many hysterical traits mixed in—growing from a need to call attention to himself, to make himself more important than he is." According to Abrahamsen, Berkowitz's motive in killing the women was to prove his power over them. He was driven by "strong, repressed sexual urges. He was afraid of women and afraid of being rebuffed by them." He didn't dare approach them sexually. "His gun was his solution. He could overwhelmingly demonstrate his power without touching them, without being rebuffed."[2]

But even if we accept Abrahamsen's analysis of Berkowitz's motive as valid, it does not explain the need to kill. Following my reasoning on narcissistic disturbances, I would assume that Berkowitz harbored a murderous rage against women, which was denied and suppressed. Under stress, however, he exploded. His controls broke down, the rage surfaced, and he went out to kill. At that time, he could hardly be described as sane.

Quite frequently now one reads or hears a new item about someone going berserk and killing a number of strangers, toward whom there could be no personal animosity. In Florida, for instance, a man recently killed seven or eight people coldly with a shotgun. They were employees of a company that, he believed, had mistreated him. After this bloodbath, the man pedaled away calmly on his bicycle. In another case, a man took a position on a rooftop and with deadly aim killed a score of people on the street. No motive for this shooting spree was ever discovered. The man himself was shot to death by the police. He was not known to be a dangerous person previously. He just went berserk.

But how can a seemingly sane person suddenly go berserk?

It doesn't make sense. There must have been some flaw in these people's personalities, some weakness in their egos, beforehand. We might compare this to a geological fault, which lies unsuspected underground until a violent earthquake shatters the surface. We know now that earthquakes do not occur haphazardly anywhere. We can be equally sure that healthy people do not suddenly go berserk and kill.

Yet earthquakes have a trigger. What, then, are the dynamics that precipitate a seemingly sane person into insane action? Beyond the flaw in the individual's personality structure, there must be some subconscious force, that when it builds sufficient pressure breaks through in destructive action. That force is the denied feeling of anger. Because the anger is denied, it is not experienced, which would give the person some control over it. On a subconscious level, it is sensed as a potentially dangerous element, which must be kept buried. The function of guarding this dangerous force belongs to the ego. Unfortunately, there is a fault in the ego's structure, because of its dissociation from body feelings. This split characterizes the narcissistic disturbance and explains why, in severe cases, this personality structure can go berserk. It is interesting that psychopathic killers are often described as "nice" or "good" people by those who know them in their day-to-day lives. This is the façade they present to hide their feelings, but it increases their tendency to explode.

THE FLOOD OF FEELING

We have no way of knowing when an outburst will occur. When it does, however, we can trace the sequence of events. A surge of feeling rises out of the unconscious, breaks through the fault, and floods the conscious mind. The feeling is so strong that the ego is unable to control it or the ensuing behavior. Such outbursts occur to many normal people, and although the explosion is generally violent in tone, it is not overtly destructive. The person has enough sense of self or ego control to stop the action before any serious damage occurs. He is aware of what is happening. We can all "fly off the handle" momentarily, but even when we do, we maintain our grasp of reality. We know we are somewhat out of control. In disturbed persons, the eruption can be so strong that the person loses contact with reality and is unaware that he is out of control. In both cases, the ego is ovehwhelmed, but in one it is momentary while in the other it lasts for some time.

"Flooding" is the significant word. In psychology, it is used to describe the condition of a person who is overwhelmed by some feeling or excitation. The ego or perceptual mind is temporarily drowned in the torrent of sensation. Imagine a river overflowing its banks and sweeping across the surrounding countryside, obliterating the normal boundaries between land and water. In a similar way, the gush of feeling wipes out the normal boundaries of the self, making it difficult for the person to distinguish inner from outer reality. Reality becomes confused and nebulous. With a river flood, one has a sense of water everywhere with no solid ground to rest on. With a psychotic break, as this sequence of events is called, one has a similar sense of nothing solid to cling to. The person feels "at sea," utterly estranged.

Estrangement is a form of disorientation. Nothing seems familiar, and so one has difficulty orienting oneself in time and space. But estrangement need not be an unpleasant experience. The person who goes berserk is overwhelmed by rage. Yet one can also be overwhelmed by pleasurable excitement. I myself recall having that experience on two occasions. One was at the age of five, when my father took me to Coney Island's famous amusement park. I was so excited by the lights, movements, and sounds that I could not tell if I was in a fairy-tale land or somewhere real. The other instance occurred when I was about seven. I was watching my friends play a game, which struck me as very funny. I couldn't stop laughing and then, suddenly, I couldn't tell if I was awake or dreaming. It's the kind of situation where one needs to pinch oneself to see if one is awake. The pain of the pinching brings one back to a consciousness of the body, which reestablishes one's boundaries and one's sense of self.

If the overwhelming sensation is not pleasurable, however, the feeling of estrangement can be very frightening. We can be overwhelmed by sorrow as well as joy, by hate as well as love. The resulting disorientation may seem a nightmare from which one will never wake up. One has lost touch with reality, and there is no proportion.

Nevertheless, in most cases, regardless of the quality of the sensations, one returns to one's normal state when and as the flood recedes. One's boundaries become reestablished, and one's perception of reality is restored. The ego is back in control. But if the flood does not recede, if the feeling of estrangement persists, the ego will be further weakened, to the point where it can no longer regain control. Reality remains vague and uncertain. In that case, the person may need treatment to restore his or her sanity.

Recovery from a psychotic break is generally quicker if there is a discharge of the affect or feeling. Blowing off steam reduces the pressure. To the uninitiated, watching a person "blow" may be frightening. But with an experienced therapist, who understands the energy dynamics involved, the seemingly irrational and violent release of feeling can have a very positive effect on the patient. Barbara was a good example.

THE CASE OF BARBARA

Barbara was first brought to my office by her husband when she was in a state of temporary insanity. She had been hospitalized for schizophrenia some years earlier. On her initial visit to me, she was decidedly out of control, shrieking and thrashing about. I could not make any contact with her through words, so I locked my arms around her and held her in a tight grip. We rolled on the floor while she screamed and screamed. I continued to hold her. It lasted about fifteen to twenty minutes. Then, it was over, like a thunderstorm. Barbara quieted down, and I could talk to her. Quite simply, she explained, her feelings had become more than she could stand; she just had to let them out. I understood her situation. Now the storm was over, and she felt safe. She went home with her husband, and I had no anxiety about her state.

In her subsequent therapy with me, I tried to help Barbara get in touch with her feelings and express them. Both of us were aware of the latent violence in her personality. She was terrified that it might break through, that she could lose control. Yet her initial experience with me showed her that letting off steam through a temporary break was not too dangerous, and she became stronger through that experience. Over the years, she had a number of screaming fits at home, which (along with reassurance and support) helped her discharge the inner tension that had, earlier, driven her crazy. Fortunately, Barbara had no children because while such behavior could be helpful to the person, it could not be comprehended by a child who would be traumatized by exposure to such scenes. I have known Barbara now for more than twenty-five years. She has become increasingly more real, more sane, more in touch with her feelings, and more of a person. I am convinced that discharging the built-up pressure within her body contributed greatly to her health and sanity.

THE RIGHT TO BE ANGRY

In *Fear of Life*, I pointed out how the English language equates an overwhelming anger with insanity. We can use one word to denote both states—"mad." To say a person is mad may mean that person is either crazy or angry. What this tells us is that anger is not an acceptable emotion. Children are taught very early to curb their anger; often, they are punished if, in the course of an angry reaction, they hurt someone. Disputes, they are admonished, should be settled amicably and with words. The ideal is to have reason prevail over action.

But conflicts cannot always be settled amicably, with reasoning. Tempers may flare. I don't mean one has to resort to physical violence to express an angry feeling. Anger can be expressed in a look or by the tone of one's voice. One can assert with feeling, "I am angry with you." Some situations, however, do call for the physical expression of anger. If someone strikes you, it may be appropriate to strike back. If violence is used on you, you have a right to use violence in return. Without the right to strike back when one is hit, one feels powerless and humiliated. We have seen what that can do to the personality.

I strongly believe that if children were allowed to voice their anger at their parents whenever they felt they had a legitimate grievance, we would see far fewer narcissistic personalities. Giving a child this right would show a real respect for the child's feelings and selfhood. In Japan some years ago, I saw a little girl of three hitting her mother in anger. The mother stood there and took it, making no effort to stop the child or reprimand her. The Japanese, to the best of my knowledge, do not believe in disciplining children before the age of six. Up to that age, children are regarded as innocents who are to be spared the knowledge of right and wrong. After six, children are taught how to behave properly, with shame as the disciplinary weapon. Despite the latitude shown to very young children or because of it, Japanese children are known to be well behaved, obedient, and respectful toward their parents. Proper behavior for Japanese is socially determined, and personal power is never an issue in relation to children. But few American parents would permit this, because they sense, quite rightly, that to do so would undermine their power. Moreover, having denied the child the right to voice anger, the parents, too, are inhibited in expressing anger. Unable to express anger appropriately, parents resort to punishment, which they see as a legitimate exercise of parental authority. There may be a place for punishment in the upbringing of children, but in many cases, it serves as a guise for the parent's release of suppressed rage and anger. The child, being helpless and dependent, has to take it, or risk an even greater rage. What happens to the personality of a child who is subjected to such treatment?

The Case of Frank

Frank, a man in his early thirties, consulted me together with his therapist because of his inability to express feeling. He had a well-built, muscular body—the result, he told me, of growing up and working on a farm. He also informed me that he had been a wrestler in school. In many ways, Frank's story called to mind the case of David, the wrestler patient described in Chapter 4. Wrestlers, it seems, know how to take it because they have had to take it.

Frank was the oldest of five children. "As far back as I can remember," he reported, "my father's normal way of relating to me was by yelling, calling me stupid, and saying that I'd 'never amount to ape shit.' He also beat me anytime that I did something that annoyed him—at chores, at the dinner table, and even when I was sleeping. Once, when I was eleven, he beat me with a rubber hose until I collapsed on the floor thinking that he was killing me and feeling that I was going to die. My mother, who was present, said to me, 'Frank, try to be a good boy and do what your father asks you.' " Frank recited this account of the treatment he had received without any show of emotion. True, it was a consultation, and he wanted to give me the pertinent background information quickly, but his lack of feeling surprised me. I realized that he had told this story before to his therapist.

Frank's earliest memory, as he told it, was "of being huddled up and feeling afraid and seeing the colors black and red all around me." And he continued, "I recall a time when I was approximately three, feeling totally anxious, rolling on the floor while my mother was telling me that I was a bad boy. I was overwhelmed and unable to run or get away. I felt as if I was possessed by a bad spirit." These experiences, one might expect, would have undermined any young person. But Frank, like Bill, used every bit of his willpower to overcome the devastation he experienced.

"In college and graduate school," Frank recounted, "I was quite macho and unfeeling. After getting my master's degree in counseling, I worked in a mental health center. In dealing with people who were in trouble, I realized that I didn't feel good about myself. I reached a point where in talking to a patient I felt that I was looking into a mirror. I sensed that I needed therapy, but I had a difficult time admitting to myself that there was indeed something wrong with me."

Bill became a psychiatrist, Frank a counselor for disturbed persons. These accomplishments meant that all available energy was funneled into studies, leaving nothing for the feeling life. Bill denied his fear, Frank denied his problems. Fortunately, they were later able to confront their anxieties. By the time I saw Frank, he had already gone through a period of therapy, and he had some insight into his difficulties.

"I have trouble with authority figures and with patients," Frank explained. "Toward the former, I feel both terror and rage, which I now know stems from my experience with my father. With the latter, I feel superior and act as if I know it all. I have also become aware of a tremendous resistance to doing anything for myself. I can sense a powerful defiance, an 'I won't' that blocks me from any positive actions. I see now how I stop myself with a fear of failure and of success, that I lie to myself about who I am, that I can't let myself feel good for any length of time. I have difficulty allowing intimacy to develop without a mask; I suppress my rage and anger. I've experienced anxiety whenever I allow myself to be soft. I set myself up to take abuse masochistically. I feel that I am a bright person who does destructive things to himself."

I was shocked at Frank's tale of the brutality he had experienced as a child. The question arose in my mind: Why didn't he become a psychopathic killer? That he could kill I had no doubt, but, as with Bill, I was equally sure that he wouldn't act it out. He had sufficient ego control. The fault in his personality was a crack, not a schism. Despite the horror of his tale, somehow he had avoided insanity. I would guess that in his babyhood he had the love and support of his mother. Another favorable element was the absence, at least from what I could learn, of seductive behavior on the mother's part. I don't believe that Frank's sanity would have remained relatively intact had he been subject to two overwhelming forces—a father's brutal hostility *and* a mother's beguiling seductiveness.

The consultation had been arranged to see what I could do or suggest to help Frank break through to his underlying sadness and anger. He had not cried deeply in any of his previous therapies. For Frank, to cry was to admit that he could not take it. It was by proving that he could take it that he defeated his father. His father might beat him down, but he couldn't break him. But the price that Frank paid was the development of a rigid body armor that locked out tears. Moreover, his macho façade prevented any real intimacy with others and so rendered his life relatively empty.

With his background in counseling and therapy, Frank could comprehend the dynamics of his condition. Based on this understanding, I used a very simple procedure with Frank to help him cry. I had him lie over a bioenergetic stool, with his hands reaching back to a chair behind him. Lying over a stool in this position is stressful and may be painful for a person whose body is rigid. To counter the stress and pain, the person is forced to breathe more deeply. Deeper breathing charges the body energetically because it introduces more oxygen into the lungs. As a result, feelings are more easily activated.

As Frank lay over the stool, I encouraged him to make a sound, for one can't cry (sob) without sound. His next instruction was to sustain the sound until the air in his lungs was fully expelled. Letting out the air fully acts against the tendency to hold in and so facilitates the expression of feeling. As the person sustains the sound in this exercise, there comes a point, near the end of the exhalation, where the voice breaks. The sound that results is very much like a sob. Then, if the person can stay at the breaking point, a real sobbing starts. The initial sob is like a priming of the pump. Once it starts, the sobbing becomes completely involuntary, getting deeper and deeper as the suppressed feelings of sadness begin to flow. Such a release will only occur, however, if the person is ready and willing for it to happen.

Frank broke into a depth of sadness and crying that surprised me as he did this exercise. In between his sobs, he also expressed the pain and anger he felt. "How could you do it to me?" he shouted. "Oh, God! Why did you hurt me? I hate you." The crying and ranting lasted several minutes. It was truly a breakthrough for him.

But Frank also needed a fuller expression of his anger. Unless he could give in fully to his anger and experience that it would not get out of hand, he would not be free of his fear of "madness." It is not enough to acknowledge these feelings intellectually. That's equivalent to saying, "Yes, I know I am carrying a live hand grenade." The proper advice is: "Get rid of it, but in a safe place." In my view, the therapeutic situation is the proper place to express and discharge these feelings. The patient can give up control because the therapist is in control.

I ask patients to hit the bed with their fists or with a tennis racket with all the force and violence they can muster. They are also encouraged to express their feelings verbally. Another technique is to have patients twist a towel with all their strength while lying on the bed. They may accompany this action with such words as: "How could you do that to me? I hate you. I will kill you." Often the release of the suppressed rage leads to a deep sobbing, as the sadness at the loss of the self wells up and is expressed. (Analytic writers speak of this as a mourning for the lost self.) Again, to an observer, the unrestrained release of rage may be frightening. Patients who really let go look mad. But this is madness only in the sense of anger, not insanity, for the patients know what they are doing. And because their actions are ego-syntonic—that is, not against their will—they are never really out of control and can stop when they wish. In the thirty years that I have used these techniques, nothing has ever been broken in my office, and I have never been hurt. Despite the screaming, yelling, and violence, patients never feel crazy in releasing their feelings. Having accepted their feelings, they end with a sense of self-possession and a realization that the real craziness was in the fixed smile, in the "good" boy or girl pose, in the denial of feeling.

With this in mind, I asked Frank to step up to the bed. He raised his fists over his head and repeatedly hit the bed with all his force. He was giving vent to the rage in him. From the way he struck the bed, I could tell that he wanted to smash it. The blows had a destructive quality. I kept Frank hitting until he had exhausted his rage. Then I showed him how to hit more effectively, with less effort, by increasing the stretch of his arms and letting the blows come off the ground. He was amazed at the difference. He was hitting like a fighter rather than like a madman. Now he had control of his violence; he could be really angry and not just mad.

• • •

For narcissists to know themselves, they have to acknowledge their fear of insanity and to sense the murderous rage inside that they identify with insanity. But they can only do this if the therapist is aware of these elements and not afraid of them. I find it helpful to point out to my patients that what they believe is insane—namely, their anger—is in fact sane if they can accept it. In contrast, their behavior without feeling, which they regard as sane, is really crazy.

8

Too Much, Too Soon

In the preceding chapter, I proposed that insanity develops when the ego or the conscious mind is overwhelmed by a feeling it cannot integrate. Again, this concept of insanity is supported by everyday speech. If we are badgered too much, we may exclaim, "Stop it. You are driving me crazy!" Unable to stand (integrate or tolerate) the continuing irritation or provocation, we sense we are ready to explode in a rage, or madness. As I indicated, I don't believe a person becomes insane simply by being pushed to the point of explosion—provided he or she can explode. Generally, it requires a special situation to drive a person crazy.

Slow torture is one such situation. In ancient Chinese practice, for instance, people were tortured by having a drop of water fall continuously on one spot on their heads while they were immobilized. The buildup of the constant stimulation became more than they could stand, and their minds cracked. Any person can be broken by a torture that doesn't stop. One either dies or goes crazy. In the first case, it is the body that is broken; in the second, it is the spirit—the energetic connection between mind and body is split. Which of the two will happen depends on the nature of the torture, and its aim.

Torture doesn't have to be physical, in the sense of a direct attack on the body. Sound can be used to break a person's will or resistance. At certain frequencies, it can be so painful that the person cannot stand it. Fear is another way to break a person's spirit. In Dostoevski's recounting of his arrest and imprisonment together with a group of radical Russian students, the following incident occurred: At their trial, they were all sentenced to death. They were brought to the execution grounds, and several were lined up before a firing squad. Then, at the last moment, the rifles were lowered, a reprieve from the Czar was announced, and they were sent to Siberia. Yet one of the men, facing the firing squad, went raving mad. His fear was too great.

We also know that a person may become temporarily insane if deprived of all sensory stimulation. In one sensory-deprivation experiment, the subject is placed in a pool with a water temperature equal to that of the human body. There is no sound, the light is uniform, and the subject is alone. Despite every effort at self-control, the subject's mind begins to hallucinate. Without some stimulation from without, the person's boundaries become vague. Infants who are left in cribs for long periods of time without being touched will go into a state of marasmus and die. We need stimulation. But we also need a balance. Too much stimulation can be as harmful as too little.

THE EGO AND ITS PROTECTIVE SHIELD

This idea that we need protection from overstimulation was advanced by Freud years ago. Picturing the organism as a vesicle, he hypothesized: "This little fragment of living substance is suspended in the middle of an external world charged with the most powerful energies, and it would be killed by the stimulation arising from these if it were not provided with a protective shield against stimuli." And he went on to remark: "Protection against stimuli is an almost more important function for the organism than reception of stimuli."[1]

The protective shield is the skin, which Freud described as "a special envelope or membrane resistant to stimuli." We recognize this function of the skin when we speak of people as thin- or thick-skinned. The former is more sensitive than the latter to stimuli. Although these colloquial references do have a physical basis (a thin skin is more sensitive to pain), they are largely metaphoric. The issue of sensitivity is related more to the aliveness of the skin—that is, to the degree that it is energetically charged.

Biologically, the protective shield develops as a process of deadening or hardening of the surface layer. Freud noted that the "outermost surface ceases to have the structure proper to living matter; [it] becomes to some degree inorganic."[2] The shell of a mollusk is a clear example of the hardening of the surface to shield the sensitive parts of the organism. Again, colloquially, we speak of people as going into a shell when they close up and shield themselves from the world.

Psychologically, the narcissists have a thick skin. They are relatively insensitive to other people and to themselves. In contrast, schizoid personalities and schizophrenics are generally so hypersensitive that it seems as if they have no skin at all. The skin can be described as the external surface or boundary of the self. In narcissists, this demarcation line is exaggerated, creating a rigid front that serves as a defense against the world but also isolates the individual. In the narcissistic character structure, the front becomes a strong façade which stands up to pressure; the front or façade of the borderline personality, on the other hand, tends to collapse under stress. Schizophrenics, with their energetically undercharged skin, have a weak and tenuous boundary, leaving them vulnerable to being overwhelmed by forces in the environment. Their defense is to withdraw from the world.

The skin is not only a protective shield and the physical boundary of the body, it is intimately connected with the consciousness. In *The Language of the Body*, I pointed out that consciousness is a function of the surface and represents the organism's perception of the interaction between inner and outer worlds. Thus, when we close our eyes and go to sleep, thereby shutting out the external world, we lose consciousness; that is, we are not aware of ourselves, and our sensitivity to stimuli from without is greatly reduced. But this process can heighten our sensitivity to what is happening on the inside, which may be described as dream consciousness. However, if someone tapped or shook us, making us aware again of the external world, ego consciousness would return and dream consciousness would retreat, leaving us with a memory of the dream. Daydreaming also depends on a greatly diminished ego consciousness, that is, consciousness of the external world. Dream consciousness, however, only occurs in light sleep. As the person passes into deep sleep, that consciousness, too, is lost. A general anesthetic brings about the same loss of consciousness. If the sleep of anesthesia is deep enough, the loss of consciousness extends to the body, too, and we do not perceive pain. In this condition, a surgeon can operate without the person feeling any pain.

A boundary or surface separates two areas of phenomena, each of which can act upon the boundary. Thus, the membrane of a cell is influenced by events in the cell as well as by events in the fluid environment about the cell. The skin is the immediate surface of the body separating the two worlds, inner and outer, and as such, it is sensitive to stimuli from without and impulses from within. Actually, the surface of the body may be said to involve not only the skin but the subcutaneous tissues and the envelope of voluntary muscles that surround the body. All our sense organs, which increase our sensitivity to events in the outer world, are located at the surface of the body. If we decrease this sensitivity, we decrease ego consciousness. For example, by freezing the surface of the skin, one can induce a local anesthesia, reducing consciousness in that area. But as we saw earlier, ego consciousness can also be reduced by a general anesthetic that acts directly upon the brain or brain stem, blocking the perceptive functions of that organ. So two surfaces are involved in ego consciousness: the surface of the body and the surface of the brain. And two events are necessary, therefore, for consciousness or awareness to occur: An event occurring within or without the organism must make an impact upon the surface, and perception or recognition of that impact must take place in the brain. Perception is an ego function and is located on the surface of the brain, which acts like a radar or television screen on which a picture develops of what is happening. In the same way, the surface of the body acts like the antenna of a television which receives the signals before they are projected upon the screen as an image.

We can think of consciousness as a light in the darkness of the unconscious which enables us to see. But we can only see that which is in our field of vision or upon which the light shines. In this sense, consciousness is more like a searchlight illuminating only a small area and leaving the rest in an even greater darkness. In like fashion, a radar can only make out objects which are in the direction and range of its signals.

Imagine consciousness, then, as a revolving beacon that lights up events in the outer and the inner world. The two are never in the beam of consciousness at the same time. If we focus on the external world, we decrease our awareness of our inner world and vice versa. And here there is a marked contrast between the consciousness of the narcissist and the schizoid personality. The narcissist focuses sharply on external reality to the relative exclusion of the inner world of feeling. The schizoid personality, on the other hand, withdraws from the external world into an inner reality. Schizophrenic withdrawal indicates that the individual cannot cope with the forces and pressures of the external world. Narcissists, on the other hand, can cope rather well, although they are unable to respond emotionally to situations. What they do is manipulate people and things, for they have reduced all objects to images. The schizophrenic, too, functions in terms of images, often highly charged emotional ones, but they have little relation to the reality of the outer world. Normal persons also conceive of reality in terms of images that are emotionally charged, but they correspond to reality. People are not *reduced* to images.

Consciousness is both an active and a passive function. We cannot turn the light of consciousness on deliberately, but once we are conscious, we can direct the light where we wish or where our interest lies. Generally, however, we leave ourselves open to see and sense what is around. That part of consciousness which is active, both in perception and response, constitutes the ego. The ego enables us to consciously change our environment to meet our needs or to adapt ourselves to our environment. Through the ego, we remove an obstacle from our path, and if that can't be done, we modify our behavior to get around the barrier. In my opinion, however, people have become all too egotistic in modifying nature to meet their needs and altering their own natures to meet alleged obstacles. We are, for instance, the only animals who will deny our feelings in the pursuit of power. In this, we have gone against our nature.

But how can one turn against one's nature? Freud pointed out that normally there is no shield against excitations arising from within the organism. These excitations are perceived as pleasure or pain or as impulses associated with emotions, feelings, and sensations. Not to perceive these excitations places a serious handicap on the organism's ability to survive and fulfill itself. It can happen, however, that internal excitations arise which, in Freud's terms, "produce too great an increase in unpleasure: there is a tendency to treat them as though they were acting, not from the inside, but from the outside, so that it may be possible to bring the shield against stimuli into operation as a defense against them."[3] Freud is saying that painful feelings can be denied access to consciousness.

Shielding the organism against stimuli it cannot handle is part of the ego's adaptive function, designed to protect the integrity of the person. Thus, the ego may even deny some aspects of external reality as a means of defense. We have seen this in patients who described their childhood as happy and their parents as loving despite their own admission of traumatizing beatings, punishments, and criticisms. To survive in such a situation, children have to suppress their rebellion and submit, which they can only do by denying their own feelings and the reality of their parents' behavior. But this valid defense becomes a neurosis when it is continued into adulthood and operates in situations in which the person is not helpless.

Since denial is achieved by deadening the surface to stimuli, its effect is to rigidify the ego. The constant smile becomes a mask one can no longer remove. The result is a diminishing of the ego's capacity to respond emotionally to reality or to change reality in line with one's feelings. To expand on Freud's analogy, the rigid ego is like a rigid rider on a horse, vulnerable to being thrown by any strong upsurge of movement (feeling). The ego's safety lies in a deadened body, with little emotion. Yet this very deadness creates a hunger for sensation, leading to the hedonism typical of a narcissistic culture.

In sum, a person gets into serious trouble if he or she is

overstimulated without any channel to release the excess excitation. That excitation is experienced as pain or unpleasure, as Freud put it, because of the intense pressure for release. When this tension reaches the point where the person can no longer stand the pain, the person anesthetizes him- or herself. The ego uses its shield against stimuli to block its perception of the inner torment. The greater the threat of discharge, then, the more energy is invested in the façade presented to the world, which is the person's way of controlling and denying feeling. The final effect of overstimulation is to imprison the true, feeling self.

OVERLOADING IN DAY-TO-DAY LIFE

Overstimulation is a general condition in the cities of the Western world. There is too much noise, too much movement, too much activity, too much unusual stimulation. The noise in a large city like New York is almost unbelievable. It is a form of pollution destroying the quiet and peace. However exciting all the sounds may be at first, the constant level of auditory input soon becomes disturbing. It's enough to drive one crazy. How do New Yorkers stand it? We all know the answer. They deaden themselves to it. They close off and don't really hear the noise. As awareness is a function of contrasts, they only realize how noisy the city is when, on a Sunday morning, the buzz of activity slows and a relative quiet takes over.

The movement in a large city, both vehicular and pedestrian, has a similar effect. At first it seems exciting, but in the end it is too much. As if in a torrential outpouring, the crowd of moving people catches one up in its current and sweeps one along in its rush. One loses the sense of oneself as a feeling being. The pace is too fast; one doesn't have time. It is dehumanizing. As if to remind me of what had been lost, recently I woke to a beautiful Sunday morning in New York. It was fall, and the air was crisp and clean. There were few automobiles, and the hustle and bustle of commercial activity was absent. I felt a keen pleasure walking the streets, a pleasure I knew from my youth growing up in the city, but one that I rarely experience anymore. New York had a human quality in those days.

It is difficult to appreciate the degree of change that has occurred in this century. Horse-drawn streetcars were still in existence at the turn of the century. Men with brooms swept the gutters. My father used to go to the local barbershop each morning for a shave and to hear the gossip. It cost him five cents. I don't have that luxury. The difficulty in appreciating the change is because we have adapted ourselves to the new conditions so well that they seem natural. But we pay a price for this adaptation to the stress of modern life, and that price is the erection of barriers to shield us from the overstimulation. To function at the pace of a machine, we have to become like a machine, which means we have to deaden our bodies and deny our feelings.*

Overstimulation isn't only in the cities. It occurs in all kinds of homes. In many American homes, the radio and television are turned on for long periods of time. It is reported that the average American watches six hours of TV a day. Many women and men watch TV or listen to the radio while doing household tasks or even outdoor chores. It seems they need this stimulation; it adds an excitement to their lives which seems to be lacking. But TV and radio also serve as distractions—they take one out of oneself and distance one from one's feelings. The news on radio and TV is

* *Overload* by Leopold Bellak describes the same condition, which he attributes to overstimulation due to constantly changing events. Overloading reduces the individual's ability to cope with new situations except in a superficial manner.[4]

particularly disturbing because often feelings are provoked that cannot be expressed. Hearing about a vicious crime can arouse an anger that has no outlet for discharge. One soon learns not to be affected, but this means one has strengthened the shield against stimuli.

Yet another factor adding to the overstimulation is the constant activity demanded by Western society. There seems to be so much to do that it is almost impossible to stop—to rest, to think, to contemplate. Just to get through a day's work one has to keep moving all the time. People are busy either making money or spending money or taking care of the things they buy. And think about driving an automobile. Not only is it stressful because of the need to be alert, but you are also constantly bombarded by the changing views.

And yet people seem to need all this activity. There may be too much to do, but too little leaves them bored and restless. They need projects to provide some excitement, so as soon as one thing is finished, another is started. The young people of today have been called the action generation, implying a virtue in their constant activity. Their restlessness, however, stems from an inability to be still. They feel alive only when they are *doing*, but their doing is a defense against *being* and feeling.[5] Among these young people, there are some who move faster than others, who strive to go up the ladder of the world more quickly. They are called the "fast-trackers." Everything in their lives is subordinated to their drive for success.

It is not an accident that the loud sounds of rock music have become the fashion. Together with strobe lights, they provide stimulation powerful enough to penetrate almost any shield and excite the viewer-listener. But excitement is not enough, one needs the pleasure of discharge. This is provided by the heavy, rhythmic beat and the intense movements of disco dancing. Such a setup seems to provide a sense of aliveness to the narcissistic individual. But rock music and disco dancing also further the narcissist's inner deadness by making overstimulation seem a normal way of life. That is the real danger of overstimulation. Having adapted to it, we do not seem to be able to do without it.

OVERSTIMULATION IN THE FAMILY

Although I believe the narcissistic disorder is a product of Western culture, I also believe the narcissistic individual is a product of an unhappy family situation, in which the child is seduced into a special relationship with one parent (see Chapter 5). Through the intimacy provided by that relationship, the child is exposed to and overstimulated by adult feelings and adult sexuality. The parent may turn to the child for sympathy and understanding and even share with the child his or her feelings of frustration with the spouse. How can a child handle such powerful emotional appeals? A parent's distress is always too much for a child. There is nothing the child can do.

Marital stress is often compounded by the hurts, disappointments, and frustrations in both partners' childhoods. Unable to respond to each other's distress, the couple may turn to their children for the love they didn't get from their parents. Regardless of how they treat the children, there is always a demand, stated or unstated: "Tell me how much you love me; tell me what a good parent I am." How often does a parent make a child feel guilty with the remark "See how much I struggle for you"? Of course, the child is aware of the parent's struggle, for the child can sense the parent's pain. As one patient said, "My mother's sadness was overwhelming. I couldn't bear to see her sorrow. I had to do everything in my power to make her happy." Her experience is not unique. Unfortunately, it is rather common.

Let us say that it is the mother who comes to the child with her problems. What can a child do to make his or her mother happy? The first thing is to be "there" for her—to listen to her tales of woe, to sympathize with her suffering, to understand her difficulties. The child has to be "there" for her as her mother wasn't. In effect, the child becomes a parent to the parent. How many times have I heard my female patients remark, "I was a mother to my mother." The boy may be more like a husband, taking the place of a "good father." But nothing changes. The mother continues her masochistic whining, complaining, and cajoling. The child feels inundated with unpleasant feelings, which he or she can do nothing about. The child cannot even leave. The only thing the child can do is not to make any demands on the mother—to suppress his or her own needs and feelings so as not to make mother feel guilty for her lack of attention.

The feelings aroused in children by such a situation are pain, sadness, and rage, both for themselves and their parents. Because these feelings are more than children can handle, they must evoke the protective shield against them, they must not let themselves feel. If they felt fully, they would scream out their pain, sob their sadness, and strike out with a destructive fury. But they do not do this—that would seem crazy. Their solution is to armor themselves, to tense the muscles of their bodies so that any expression of feeling is impossible. They have put themselves into a psychological straitjacket.

Armoring takes several forms on the body level, all of which reflect a degree of overall rigidity. The expression "armoring" was introduced by Wilhelm Reich to describe a process whereby chronic tension develops in the superficial muscles of the body to form a hard shield against insult from without and impulse from within. In some narcissistic individuals, the body has a statuesque appearance because of the rigidity. In other cases, the body may have a massive, blocklike quality, as if the rigidity were designed to resist pressure. One patient described his mother as a tank. His own body impressed me as being like a concrete pillbox. This was his way of armoring against the tank. Yet in many cases, as we have seen, the body is not armored in the sense of an overall rigidity. Still, there is a band of tension at the base of the skull, which serves to split perception from body events.

So far, in discussing overstimulation by the parents, I have spoken rather generally. I believe the real overstimulation is sexual. I mentioned that seduction always has sexual overtones, no matter how innocent the parent's actions may seem. Alice Miller, an eminent European psychoanalyst, comments:

> A father who grew up in surroundings inimical to instinctual drives may first dare to look properly at a female genital, play with it, and feel aroused while he is bathing his small daughter. A mother [who has developed a fear of the male genital] may now be able to gain control over her fear in relationship to her tiny son. She may, for example, dry him after his bath in such a manner that he has an erection which is not dangerous or threatening for her. She may massage her son's penis right up to puberty in order to "treat his phimosis."[6]

According to Miller, such parental actions will make a child insecure about sexuality, and this is increased by parental prohibition of the child's own autoerotic activities. I think "insecurity" is a mild word to describe the effects of such sexual overstimulation. Let us remember that a child who is stimulated sexually by a parent has no possibility of discharging the excitation. George's case may be extreme, but it illustrates the problem clearly.

George, who had been one of my patients, underwent some deep muscle massage. Afterward, he wrote me:

> He [the masseur] said my skull was like a coconut, my jaw was like I was chewing on nails, my neck had a noose around it, my chest was underinflated, my ass was tight as a drum, and my knees

were stiff. On an ego level I understood a lot of what happened to me. Something terrorized me, and I built a suit of armor around it. Sexually, when I was young, my father used to slap me between the legs and say, "Get the chicks." I used to sleep between my mother and sister. Very anxiously I ran my hands all over my sister's body, but I only touched the top half of my mother's body. This was before I masturbated.

My sister took me to horror movies. I was terrified watching horror shows on TV with my father. I used to lie in my bed motionless for long periods of time with my head under the cover, afraid to look at the door. I thought if someone came through the door, I would go crazy.

I am afraid to put my arms around my mother because sleeping between her and my sister started me closing off sexually. I am afraid it will happen again. I am so frozen I sit in a chair with her for hours without saying anything.

George's words highlight the harm that can be done to a boy when he is overstimulated sexually and at the same time terrified of his father because of the Oedipal situation. George couldn't resist touching his mother and sister because it was too exciting, but he couldn't enjoy it because he felt too guilty and too frightened. It was torture. All he could do was clench his jaw, tighten his body, and try to stand it. This meant closing off his feelings, particularly sexual ones. He is still afraid to touch a woman and can only have oral sex with prostitutes.

Almost all children are exposed today to too much sexual stimulation both in the home and in the environment. Some parents think it is smart to walk around the house naked in front of their children. They imagine it will prevent the development of sexual inhibitions in the child. They do not realize that it is a sexual exposure and not nudity. In a culture where people regularly wear clothes, taking them off has a sexual implication. (This implication is absent in a nudist camp, where no one wears clothes.)

Too many children in modern culture grow up too quickly. A good example is a friend's daughter who demanded at age four that she be fitted with tight jeans so she could show off her body. Unfortunately, some parents take pride in the precocious development of their children and even encourage it. But the seeming maturity of these precocious children is only a sophistication. They are intellectually advanced but emotionally retarded. The exposure of young children to adult sexuality may reduce inhibition to acting on one's impulses, but it will also reduce sexual feelings.

Ruth was such a person—an attractive young woman, seemingly quite sure of herself. She had a degree in psychology and was engaged in a doctoral program. Yet when I looked at her body at a bioenergetic workshop, I was shocked. It was the body of a fifteen- or sixteen-year-old girl, and Ruth was thirty-three years old. I could picture her body looking twenty years old when she was past forty. It made me think of Dorian Gray. Ruth didn't grow older because she didn't grow up. On some deep level, she still remained a child. Her mind was adult and quite alert, but her body remained undeveloped because its life, its emotions, had been denied and suppressed. Ruth's sense of self was split. Sometimes she felt like an old woman; at other times she felt she hadn't lived yet.

Patricia was another example. When she walked into my office for a consultation, I was struck by her air of self-possession, confidence, and poise. She was only twenty years old, but she talked like a woman of the world, referring nonchalantly to her use of cocaine and drunken binges. Patricia did admit she was in trouble—she couldn't concentrate, and she couldn't do her college work. I realized that her seeming sophistication was a façade; inwardly she was still a child. When she dropped her front for a minute, I could see the child in her eyes. Patricia described herself as special. Her father and her teachers had always told her that she was better than the other girls. And she had excelled at tennis, swimming, and riding—it was expected of her. But after puberty, her performance in these activities declined. She was still popular because she was attractive and put on a good show, but it was all show and no feeling. She couldn't cry, shout, or scream. In fact, she was embarrassed by any expression of feeling.

Patricia had engaged in sex, so I asked her about her experiences. "I don't think it's all that it's cracked up to be," she replied. "I don't think it's that important." At twenty! But her remark is understandable in the light of the tension in her pelvis. There was no feeling. The lower part of her body was so tightly contracted that any free or spontaneous movement was almost impossible. The sexual act was meaningless, even when she cared for the young man. What a tragic situation for a young woman!

The bodies of many young men also show a degree of immaturity that contrasts with an old facial expression. The difference is even more marked when a beard is worn. By contrast, the small pelvis and thin legs have a boyish quality. In some cases, the upper part of the body also looks youthful because of a narrow chest. And this young look may even flicker across the grown-up face, especially if the man smiles or the beard is removed. Some mature men may manifest a boyish quality that is very charming, but that is different. The men I am describing are both old and young at the same time—intellectually sophisticated but emotionally immature.

These young people, men and women, are emotionally fixated in early youth because their development was arrested. They lost their childhood innocence too soon and with it the opportunity for a playful and carefree existence that would allow a slow, natural maturation of their faculties. They are pushed to learn with educational toys and games under the watchful eyes of parents who are constantly measuring their progress. Children need to be left alone to play for the pure pleasure of it, without any ulterior purpose such as learning. And children sense the parents' expectations, whether they are explicitly stated or not. Too often parents look only to a child's achievements, to signs of "specialness" in the world. They follow a child's progress as fans follow a team's. How well is the child doing at school, in sports, with friends? Failure is not acceptable. But there are also many parents who are aware of the tremendous competitive pressure today's culture places on children, and they try to assure their children that being average is good enough. Unfortunately, it is very difficult for a child who has been made to feel special at home to accept being average or common in the world. No one can be free from cultural forces. In the Western world, which is oriented to material success, failure is the major sin.

TOO LITTLE NURTURING

Another reason for the pressure on children to grow up fast is the desire of parents to be free from the burden of always being "there" for the child. They want to devote more energy to their own need for personal fulfillment. This move may seem reasonable from the parent's point of view, but the way it is done today is counterproductive. The absence of a mother does have a negative effect on the child, for a mother is the child's primary world, especially when breast-feeding is considered. In my opinion, it is contact with the mother's body that is particularly important in the early years. I don't believe that a father can substitute for a mother in this respect; his body lacks a quality of softness that hers has. Admittedly, one may have to support a mother's desire to get away from her children to promote her health and good feelings, on which the child is dependent. Yet it is sad to me when the needs of a mother conflict with those of her children.

It is important not to be caught in the narcissism of our culture that identifies personal fulfillment with success in the world of affairs. There is an ego satisfaction to be obtained from such success, but it does not fulfill the basic needs of the individual nor his or her potential for being. The basic needs are body needs and can only be fulfilled on a body level. They are to breathe fully and deeply, to eat with a hearty appetite, to sleep when one is tired, and to make love with a passionate desire. What is the good of being successful, achieving a name, if one is sick and miserable in one's being? I once treated a successful author who was so depressed that he woke each morning with the desire to die. One is most fulfilled in one's being when one is most alive, vibrantly alive. Fulfillment is in the full use of all our faculties. It is narcissistic to think that we are only fulfilled through the use of our minds. Not to enjoy the use of our legs to walk, our arms to hold, our eyes to see, our lips to kiss, is to be deprived, not fulfilled. Doesn't this argument apply to a woman's breasts, which were designed to nurse a baby? What can be more fulfilling than nourishing a new life?

I am not against women having careers or achieving success. They have the same creative potential as men and can offer as much to the world. But I don't believe that a man or woman is fulfilled by what he does. A person finds his true fulfillment in being, not doing, in being the kind of person who through his own good feelings can help others to feel good, too. One's accomplishments are the icing on the cake, the gravy on the meat. Only narcissists confuse the dressing with the meal. My argument here is that if we do not fulfill the needs of our children, we predispose them to a narcissistic personality disorder.

Children need nurturing in the form of love, support, closeness, and contact with the mother's body to develop a full and secure self. They also need attention and respect for their feelings in order to gain a solid sense of self. If these are deficient, the child will have a feeling of unfulfillment that will continue on into adulthood. Such a person as a mother would see the child's needs and demands as an obstacle to her own personal fulfillment. As a result of this conflict, she would have difficulty fulfilling her child's needs, and so the problem of unfulfillment gets passed on from one generation to another.

The very conditions of modern life may pose obstacles to proper nurturing. This was clearly brought out to me on a flight from New York to Detroit. It was an early (7:30 A.M.) departure. I sat next to a mother with two daughters, one aged two and a half, the other nine months. The older child wore a tee shirt with the inscription "Liberated Woman." Although not a woman, she had been "liberated" from her childhood by the demands of the situation. The plane was crowded, the mother was preoccupied with the baby, so the little girl had to behave like an adult. But she couldn't quite make it; she was restless. The mother told me that they had all gotten up at 5:30 A.M. to make the plane. But that didn't excuse the child. When she disturbed her mother, she was told, "Sit quietly. Do you want me to spank you again?"

I felt sorry for this little girl. Despite my awareness of the difficult situation the mother was in, I couldn't warm toward her, especially when she told me, in reference to the little girl, "She has made this trip a number of times." The mother said this with pride, as if that fact denoted a degree of maturity and sophistication in the child. Whatever the reasons for these trips, and they may have been important, the child suffered through them. For example, she never cried, though I could see that she was close to it several times. Although I sensed that the mother was a warm person, with a deep love for her daughters, in the conflict between her interests and the children's, the latter were sacrificed. The incident was suggestive of how little room and time a mother may have in her busy life for her feelings or her children's. Travel or some other activity takes precedence over feelings.

The main effect of too little nurturing on a child is the suppression of the feeling of longing, specifically, longing for contact with the mother's body, which represents love, warmth, and security. The feeling is suppressed because it is too painful to want desperately something one cannot have. But without this feeling it is difficult to become close and intimate physically with another human being on a feeling level. All narcissists have this problem, and it cannot be resolved until the feeling of longing is reactivated. Longing is expressed in reaching out with the arms to hold someone and with the lips to kiss the person. Kissing is an extension of the baby's sucking the breast. The feeling of longing, then, is suppressed by inhibiting the impulse to reach out and suck—by compressing the lips, clenching the jaw, and contracting the throat. By these tensions, the child, in effect, says, "I won't want you, Mommy, because I can't have you."

Sucking is wanting on its deepest level because sucking is taking in. When we breathe, we suck in air. If one's sucking is inhibited, one's breathing is disturbed, becoming shallow rather than full and deep. Many people restrict their breathing because deep breathing energizes the organism and leads to feeling. The most immediate way to block a feeling is to hold one's breath.

Shallow breathing is reflected in the restriction of the respiratory movements to the diaphragm area. In deeper breathing, both the throat and abdomen are involved, and the process of sucking in air is more active and aggressive. The throat opens, literally becoming bigger, and the abdominal wall moves outward, expanding that cavity. Psychologically, opening the throat opens the way to the heart and its feelings, expressed in the sounds of singing and crying.

Closing the throat allows nothing in or out. Sucking can also be shallow or deep, like breathing. One can suck with the lips and tongue or with the tongue pressing against the hard palate, the back of the mouth, and the throat. Bottle-fed babies suck in a superficial manner, whereas breast-fed babies suck with the back of the mouth, the nipple against the hard palate.

When patients are encouraged to breathe deeply by sucking in air with the throat, it not infrequently has a dramatic effect. After a number of such breaths, patients may quite spontaneously break into deep sobbing. Sometimes, too, they feel the pain of frustrated longing in their throats. If at the same time they are asked to reach out with lips and arms, as a baby might to the mother, they may experience the deprivation of nurturing they suffered as a child. In most cases, however, the patient is strongly defended against feeling the pain and sadness of this deprivation, and it requires considerable therapeutic work to bring up these suppressed feelings.

THE CASE OF KAREN

Karen came to therapy because, as she put it, she had no feelings. She felt almost nothing in her body and functioned like a mechanical doll. Her mouth and throat were especially contracted, and she had so little sensation in her lips that a kiss meant nothing to her. "Two mouths meeting is like a foreign thing to me," she commented. She had no desire for any intimate contact with another human being.

Karen's childhood could be described as a nightmare. She had very little physical contact with her mother and almost none with her father, who found women disgusting. The expression of disgust engraved on his face repelled Karen; she reacted to him as he did to her. With her mother, on an emotional level, there was what I would call pseudocontact, for the mother saw Karen only as an image. "She was insane," Karen recollected. "She watched my every move. She was so 'into' me. I was her little girl. I had to be perfect."

Karen became a typical narcissist, of the borderline variety. On the surface she looked normal, but she was only a smiling doll. Inside she had little feeling. "At an early age," she related, "I couldn't be there. I couldn't take anything in. I couldn't absorb what I read; I couldn't learn at school. I couldn't breathe." Her throat was closed off.

I worked with Karen for a long time, making slow but steady progress. Feeling came back only little by little. She was aware that she had been in a state of living death; it was a long way back to life. At the beginning of therapy, it was almost impossible for Karen to cry or scream. She couldn't get any emotional sound out of her throat. We worked hard together to mobilize her body through exercises and manipulations, and eventually, after several years, she got in touch with some anger and sadness. As the therapy progressed, Karen continued to feel better, but she denied that she had any desire to be close to or intimate with another person, particularly a man. Her vagina was as unalive and insensitive as her mouth.

Karen's resistance to wanting closeness had several determinants. First of all, she was spiteful. Having been denied closeness as a child, she wasn't going to ask for it now. Her bitterness closed her up. Moreover, Karen was arrogant—men were not worth reaching for; she herself was special. I worked with these psychological defenses as they came out in the transference situation, but I couldn't get through to Karen's wanting, because under her ego defenses was pain—a pain so intense that she didn't dare feel it. This pain was connected to the longing locked up in her throat.

Finally, one session, the breakthrough of the pain occurred. Karen was working to open her throat by consciously trying to suck in as if she were gasping for air. As she did this, I applied some pressure with my fingers to the very tight scalene muscles alongside her neck. She began to cry, more deeply than ever before. In between bursts of crying and sobbing, she voiced her feelings. "My throat is so tight I can't release it just by crying," she began. As her throat finally started to open, she asked, "Why does my throat hurt now?" With each release of feeling, her crying became deeper and more intense. At one point, recalling how she had felt so alone and so desperate as a child, Karen cried out, "The pain was so total. It was the pain. The pain. It went on for years. The needing and the pain. The needing and the pain. Always needing and always the pain. How long can you go on?" As she said this, she was holding her throat while lying on the bed. She continued, "I needed you so much. And I hurt so much. There was no one to share it with, no one to tell it to. It was a total aloneness."

Karen then related an incident she had not told me about before. "I met a man who came with me to my apartment, just to have sex with me," she reported. "I was so lonely, so desperate for some physical contact. However, I couldn't respond to him sexually, so he got up and left. I was so devastated as he walked out of my apartment that I picked up some article from the table, ran after him into the hall, and said, 'I have something to give you.' He looked at me as if I were crazy and kept on going. After that experience I never needed anyone again. Something in me closed up. I would get up in the morning and go to work like an automaton. I was really insane."

As Karen lay on my couch, she sobbed deeply and loudly in bursts of feeling. In between the sobs, she wailed. It was like the wailing of an insane person. But Karen wasn't insane. She knew what she was doing. She was in touch with reality—the reality of an almost intolerable pain. It had taken many years of therapy for her to gain the courage and ego strength to confront that reality. The pain had been enough pain to drive a person crazy, so to retain her sanity, Karen had numbed herself to the *pain*. The result was an inability to breathe deeply. As she herself remarked on one occasion, "I've felt the tightness in my throat and chest for years; I felt I couldn't breathe. I couldn't get a simple, deep breath; there was much pain in my diaphragm. I don't know how I survived."

• • •

As we have seen, too much stimulation or too many demands on a child, coupled with too little nurturing and support, increase the risk of severe narcissistic disorder. Unfortunately, that is the direction modern culture is going with respect to the upbringing of children. In my opinion, career mothers don't have the time to do the job of mothering that children need. Although I do not claim that breast-feeding can prevent a child from becoming neurotic or narcissistic, it does fulfill the child's needs for closeness, contact, and erotic satisfaction. It gives the infant the feeling that mother (the infant's world) is "there." But how many mothers today can devote themselves fully to their children? Some are themselves deprived, looking for their own fulfillment. How much easier to feed the child with prepared baby foods! And if the child is restless, they find some way to distract the child with toys. I have known parents who drove their children about in a car to quiet them down for a nap. It seems that the more active the culture becomes, the less time there is for children, who are, then, more deprived. It is a vicious circle, for deprived children seek their fulfillment in a restless activity that leaves them more frustrated. Is it any wonder that so many turn to drugs? Drugs are one way to numb the body and kill the pain. Another way is to become so busy in the worldly power struggle that one has no time to feel.

I recognize that many women go to work as a matter of

economic necessity. If that necessity is an issue of survival or even of living decently, the needs of children may have to be subordinated to that necessity. But many mothers work for a standard of living that in other times and other places would be considered luxury. Of course, people would like to have what others have, and their self-esteem may suffer if they can't keep up with the Joneses. This desire is the force that powers a narcissistic culture that, in turn, robs life of meaning and dignity and creates narcissistic individuals. However, I don't believe that the individual is just a cog in an economic machine or that he or she is just a helpless victim of a culture going insane. If that is so, then our situation is hopeless. Fortunately, therapy has shown that people have the potential to take responsibility for their lives. If each person would do that, society would change. Still, if only one person does it, we are not lost. The first step is to recognize the insanity of our times.

9

The Insanity of Our Time

THE GUISE OF SANITY

The question that concerns us is: On what grounds can we describe the state of our culture as insane? Leopold Bellak, a noted psychiatrist, psychologist, and psychoanalyst, makes the following clinical diagnosis of the modern social-psychological condition. "If being crazy means having a hard time adapting to the world as it is (a definition that I agree with), then society *is* crazy."[1] But while I agree with his diagnosis, I don't quite agree with his reasoning. If the world we live in, that is, the world of culture, is unreal, then an inability to adapt would not be regarded as crazy. As I see it, narcissists are perfectly adapted to the world we live in; they subscribe to its values, they flow with its constantly changing patterns, and they feel at home in its superficiality. Those of us who have a sense of the past, who seek stability and security rather than change, and who have no faith in computer systems have real difficulty adapting. I find it personally disturbing every time the price of a common product changes as a result of inflation. Who is crazy and why?

In courts of law, as we saw in Chapter 7, there is no such thing as a little crazy. A patient is judged either sane or insane. This decision is necessary to determine whether a person should be held responsible for a crime and sent to prison, or if the person should be hospitalized. But this either-or position doesn't fit the commonsense point of view, which recognizes that such things are rarely black or white, that people can be partly crazy even if they seem to function normally. I am a great believer in common sense because it represents the accumulated experience of a lot of people. Thus, I also agree with the commonsense idea that self-destructive behavior must be considered insane. Narcissistic behavior falls in this category.

What can we say about the nature of insanity? As I have already mentioned, overt insanity can be guaged by a person's lack of contact with reality, usually shown by a disorientation in time and space. Psychiatrists may ask: "Do you know what day this is? Do you know who you are? Where you are?" The inability to answer these questions correctly is rather clear proof of disorientation, of a loss of contact with reality, and therefore of insanity.

But if a person is out of touch with his feelings, is he out of contact with reality? If an individual is identified with his image or false self, does he really know who he is? If he believes that without power one will be used and humiliated, is he not a little insane? In other words, is there a degree of insanity in the narcissistic personality?

Recall that in the first chapter I described a spectrum of narcissistic disturbances. That spectrum included the paranoid personality, in whom we find the presence of megalomania. But megalomania is not limited to paranoid individuals. It can be found on some level in all schizophrenics. A mental patient who believes himself to be Jesus Christ or Napoleon sees himself in the most grandiose terms. Every schizophrenic has an inflated self-image, which is out of touch with reality. But isn't every inflated self-image unreal? And if that is so, isn't grandiosity itself an expression of unreality and therefore a mark of some degree of insanity?

The question that arises here, as it has in other parts of

this study, is the following: If the narcissist is insane to some degree and if the schizophrenic is narcissistic, what is the difference beween them and what relation do they have to each other? One criterion is that given by Bellak, namely, the ability to cope. The schizophrenic can't adapt or cope with his environment, whereas the narcissist can. Of course, his coping is on a superficial level, but on that level it is effective and serves, therefore, as a hold on reality or a defense against an underlying insanity. This concept can be extended to all neurotics since there is some measure of narcissism in every neurotic individual. This means that there is also an element of schizophrenia in all neurotics.[2] However, clinical diagnoses are often based on the outstanding symptomology, with the result that schizoid and narcissistic tendencies that are in the background of the personality are generally ignored.

To the degree that one's identity is based on an image, one is not in contact with the reality of one's being. In all other respects, the individual may appear to be oriented and fully in contact with reality, but there is in his or her personality a fracture—maybe only a hairline break—that constitutes a tendency to insanity. As the degree of narcissism increases, the break becomes more pronounced, but it still lies below the surface and can be easily covered over. Thus, the spectrum of narcissism can be seen also as a scale of insanity. At one end are the phallic-narcissists, whose behavior is so attuned to Western culture that their sanity would not be questioned; at the other end are the manifestly insane paranoid schizophrenics. In between are the narcissistic characters, borderline personalities, and psychopathic personalities.

Let us look at psychopathic personalities. At times their behavior can be so bizarre and so self-destructive that one readily questions their sanity. Yet on inquiry, one finds that they are fully oriented to the situation, their cognition is not disturbed, and their responses seem logical and convincing. The idea of an underlying insanity in the psychopathic personality is the thesis by Hervey Cleckley, professor of psychiatry, entitled *The Mask of Sanity*.[3] His book contains a number of detailed case histories of persons whose behaviors are clearly psychopathic, involving lying, stealing, forgery, drunkenness, vulgar public display, and sexual promiscuity. The amazing thing about these individuals is that by talking and listening to them, one would not believe the documented record of their actions. They impress the interviewer as sincere, honest, alert, intelligent, and perceptive.

The Records of Anna and John

Cleckley describes the case of Anna, a woman who, at forty, gave an impression of energy, playful spontaneity, and radiant youth. Her composure and manner suggested good breeding and education. She spoke simply but intelligently and quite knowledgeably about many subjects. Cleckley comments that even knowing Anna's record, one would be inclined to dismiss it in view of the "obvious character of this appealing woman."

To appreciate the record, one must know that Anna was born in the first decade of the twentieth century to wealthy parents in Georgia. This means that Anna was brought up to be a "lady," decked out in white gloves and a stylish hat. The record begins when Anna was an adolescent in the local high school. A club of ten boys formed to share their experiences of Anna's sexual favors. When this became known publicly, her parents were aghast and sent her away to boarding school. Her conduct there, however, eventually led to her dismissal. Starting with minor violations such as smoking, cutting classes, and being disrespectful, she went on to lying, cheating, and petty thievery. This pattern was continued at the more than half a dozen schools she attended. There was a devil in Anna which seemed to delight in shocking people. At one school, she placed condoms around the cushions of sofas in the room where boys and girls were allowed to meet, in such a way that they would be exposed as the young people moved about. I suppose no one would be shocked by this today, but Anna's culture was still Victorian. At another school, she wrote on the door of the office of the sedate Latin teacher: HOT PUSSY AVAILABLE HERE—CHEAP

On leaving school, Anna engaged in a career of sexual promiscuity, including various pickups in bars and on the streets, and occasionally gang banging. After drinking at a local hot spot, she and a group of men would ride out to the country, where each man had intercourse with Anna in turn. She was married several times to men she had no special feelings for and was never faithful to any of them. This behavior took place while Anna "passed in the community as a reliable, conforming, and attractive woman. Much of the time she seemed poised, polite, and a paradigm of happy behavior."[4] For a while, she even taught a Sunday School class. Her teaching was ethically admirable and gave a strong impression of sincerity.

The diagnosis of psychopathic personality is clear from her pattern of behavior, despite the absence of any evident striving for power or attempt at self-aggrandizement. Anna never gave any sign that she experienced any emotion in connection with her actions. Even when her sexual activities and pranks became known, she showed no shame, fear, or consternation. Of her sexual affairs, Cleckley says that most probably "this woman has somewhat less than ordinary conscious sexual motivation and that the most significant feature of her sexual experiences is that despite frequent mechanical responses, it has meant so little to her."[5]

Anna's sexual activity meant so little to her because she had no feeling. It was largely mechanical. Without feeling, she couldn't experience any guilt, shame, or remorse. But then the big question is: Why did she do it if there was no feeling? What was her motivation? Cleckley offers no answer to these questions, nor does he consider them. He does make one very significant comment about Anna. Recognizing that the normal emotions of love, hate, joy, and suffering were absent from Anna's adult personality, he remarks, "I will not say that Anna never loved or hated or suffered. I think there was a time when she probably did all of these precociously and beyond ordinary degree. All that, however, is beyond an iron curtain."[6] The iron curtain is the denial of feeling so characteristic of all narcissistic personalities.

Psychopathic acting out like Anna's can be explained psychologically as a rejection of and rebellion against parental values. Drawing on what psychoanalysis has taught us, we also explain it as a getting back at the parent who hurt her. Anna may not have felt any grief about her failure to behave as a "normal" child, but her parents may have. If they suffered from her behavior, we can assume that unconsciously this was her aim. Cleckley's remark hints at some deep hurt, a betrayal of love, in early life, to which she reacted by cutting off feeling. Perhaps her father was seductive and then rejecting when her sexual feelings surfaced. That is not uncommon. Perhaps there was hypocrisy in the family. The upright citizen, father, and husband could have been a lecher at heart. That, too, is possible.

These assumptions may explain some aspects of Anna's behavior. But they leave unanswered the question of why she acted out as she did. Before examining this question, however, let us consider another of Cleckley's cases.

According to Cleckley, John, a successful physician, was highly regarded in his community. Unlike Anna, he had made a good adjustment to life. Nevertheless, his history showed a number of purposeless misdeeds, starting in early childhood but becoming more serious as he grew older. For example, he lost several promising hospital appointments by arriving at work dead drunk or by breaking out in obscene language or behavior. He was forced to move from one town, where he had a well-established practice, because of a scandal arising from an escapade in a brothel. During a wild drinking party with a friend and two prostitutes, he bit off the nipple of one of the women. Although, by making a big settlement upon her, he avoided prosecution, he was forced to leave the area. He learned no lesson from this incident. Episodes of drinking to stupefaction in hotel rooms, breaking furniture, and calling his wife to say that he was going to kill himself continued on a regular basis. Why? What forces drove this man to such obviously self-destructive behavior? What force drives any man to drink to the point where he loses control over his actions?

THE QUESTION OF SELF-DESTRUCTIVE BEHAVIOR

To understand self-destructive behavior, we must recognize that it cannot be a nonsensical act. To regard any action as meaningless is to deny that life has an inner direction. To think that the id is chaotic or that our impulses are as haphazard as the movement of molecules contradicts common sense. A living organism is a highly organized system governed by two forceful instincts—one toward self-preservation and the other toward perpetuation of the species. Self-destructive behavior goes directly against the first of these, yet it occurs. Some people commit suicide, but they have their reasons, which are important to them. Other people sacrifice their lives in heroic deeds, suggesting that there are forces in the human personality that can be stronger than the instinct for survival. One of these forces, I believe, is the feeling that life has to make sense, that it has to have some meaning. Many people find a sufficient meaning in the prospect of pleasure. By pleasure, I do not mean self-indulgent hedonism but the good feeling that comes from health and the ability to give oneself fully to whatever activity the times may require. In these terms, a life that offers no prospect of pleasure but only the certainty of pain would not be worth living. Without other reasons or meanings to live for, a person might be tempted to end his or her life to avoid the pain and suffering. Such an action by a terminal cancer patient, for example, would make sense.

Of course one could argue that while there is life there is hope. One could also raise the ethical question of a person's right to end his or her own life. If we leave aside the merits of the action, we can say that under some circumstances, suicide makes sense—or, at least, it made sense to the person who committed the deed. From that, it follows that other forms of self-destructive behavior might be comprehensible if we knew the person's inner state. Alcoholism, for example, should be open to an interpretation similar to that of suicide—namely, that the addiction stems from an attempt to escape intolerable feelings of pain, anxiety, or frustration. Alcoholics may numb themselves so as not to feel some inner torment. Of course, the attempt fails, for the relief from alcohol is momentary and the return to reality more painful than before. All such attempts to escape from oneself must fail; the only real escape from life is death.

Besides the desire to escape from pain, self-destructive behavior has another motivation: the unconscious wish to get back at someone, to make another suffer for the hurt the person feels. "You'll be sorry" is what the suicide in effect says to family and close friends. But I don't believe this motivation is the dominant one. My work with alcoholics has convinced me that when the inner pain is eliminated, the dependence on alcohol disappears. The pain stems from unresolved emotional conflicts that have been repressed into the unconscious. Working out these conflicts is no simple or easy undertaking. There is a tremendous anger in the alcoholic, which is turned against the self through guilt. Guilt about sexual feelings and rage is probably the psychological basis for recourse to alcohol. The alcoholic, however, is not unique in this guilt. Other neurotics suffer from it, too. Moreover, the suppression of these feelings is not complete; they threaten constantly to break through. When the effort to contain these feelings reaches the point where the individual senses that he or she can no longer hold on, the person turns to drink.

What does alcohol do? It is neither a sedative nor an anesthetic, though it may decrease anxiety and sensitivity to pain. And it is not a stimulant, though it does "enliven" some people. What alcohol does is to weaken the ego's control over the body and break down superego prohibitions, thereby releasing a person from his or her inhibitions. As a result, feelings are more easily expressed—except that the perception of emotion is dulled. People may cry when in their cups but not really feel sad; they may get angry without fully being aware that they are angry. Alcohol puts a space between the person and reality, which allows a certain amount of acting out.

Let us consider the drinking of John, the physician described by Cleckley. His drinking occurred in binges—a sign of increased stress, from within or without. We are all familiar with pressure at work or at home, but inner stress is the more important. It arises when suppressed feelings threaten to erupt into consciousness. Generally, this happens when outer stress is reduced, as on weekends or holidays. It is at these times that many people drink heavily. Unable to contain or suppress the feelings, and equally unable to express them openly because of guilt, the alcoholic becomes intoxicated. As ego control breaks down, the suppressed impulses break through—minus their full emotional content.

Again, one can be violent without feeling angry; one can cry without feeling sad; one can have sexual relations without love or guilt. John acted out his hostility to women by biting off the whore's nipple, but he did not feel any hostility. At other times, he broke furniture and threatened his wife with suicide, but he didn't feel any anger toward her. Under the alcohol-induced dulling of the ego's perceptive function, John could act in a way that would be considered mad or crazy if he was sober. But he was drunk; his actions were not taken seriously by himself or by others.

In the light of this reasoning, can we imagine what John's life was like? Undoubtedly he was an unhappy man, harboring intense hostility toward women. Still, he tried to live a respectable life as a doctor and a husband. To do this, he denied his feelings, leaving his life empty and meaningless. For John, getting drunk and acting out his hostility was a way of discharging some of the inner pressure, equivalent to blowing off steam as a safety measure. It enabled him to maintain his sanity when sober. On the other hand, drunkenness can be seen as a kind of temporary insanity. It has much in common with the disorientation of a psychotic breakdown.

Anna, whose promiscuous behavior so puzzled Cleckley, suggests a similar picture. What happens if one has strong sexual feelings but an inordinate amount of guilt about them? It's enough to drive one crazy. If the guilt cannot be reduced, one can reduce the charge of the feeling by acting it out. Like John's drinking binges, Anna's promiscuity seems a means to discharge some of her inner tension. Compulsive masturbation serves the same function. It halts the buildup of an intolerable feeling.

For Anna, the choice seemed to be respectability with the risk of going crazy or acting out crazily (sexually) and protecting her sanity. Why should respectability pose this risk for Anna or John? It doesn't for everyone. It is a question of ego strength. Respectability demands control of one's behavior, and not everyone is capable of that control. According to my spectrum of narcissism, that strength varies inversely with the degree of narcissism. Thus, the phallic-narcissist has the most ego strength, the narcissistic character less, and the borderline and psychopathic personalities even less.

I believe these considerations apply to the widespread use of drugs in our time. For many people, drugs serve as an escape from an intolerable sense of emptiness and boredom in their lives. Since life without feeling is meaningless, these people resort to any drug that promises some feeling of excitement and aliveness. The hallucinogenic drugs seem to offer that, but the increase of sensation they provide is at the expense of true feeling. All drugs are selective poisons and deaden the body. It is precisely this deadening of the body that allows sensation to increase. But one can increase sensation without drugs. If we wish to heighten our perception of music, for instance, we keep still so all our awareness can be focused on the sound. The difference is that in this case we don't deaden our bodies; we just quiet them.

Some drugs, like cocaine, act differently. The "high" they produce gives the person a sense of power and control. One feels on top of the world, and as long as one uses the drug, one can maintain the feeling. Coming off cocaine, however, may be a harrowing experience. Still, cocaine may seem the drug of choice for some narcissists. Power and control are exactly what narcissists attempt to achieve through their self-image. In any case, the price is high. And I believe there is something insane in the use of drugs and in a culture that fosters this practice. That insanity is the loss of contact with the life of the body and the escape into a world of fantasy and images.

THE ABSENCE OF LIMITS

At the beginning of this book, I suggested that an absence of limits is connected with the development of narcissism in a culture. Our age is characterized by a drive to transcend limits and the desire to deny them. Limits do exist and, factually, we may recognize them. Emotionally, however, we may not accept the idea of limits. We believe or wish to believe that human potential is unlimited. Science and technology promise a future in which people will be free from many of the natural limitations that restricted their ancestors. Even now one can travel at speeds that were inconceivable when I was a boy. But it is the denial of social limits, expressed in morals or codes of behavior, that largely promotes a narcissistic attitude.

Limits derive from structure. Knowing the structure of an object, we can determine the limits of its possible action. For example, an automobile, because of its structure, can't fly like an airplane or dive like a submarine. Humans, too, are limited by their structure. Having only two legs, we can't run as fast as a horse. We can't climb trees like monkeys, swim like dolphins, or endure the cold like polar bears. Our structure, however, has a potential for movement: our hands to manipulate objects, our tongues for speech, and our faces for the expression of feeling that no other animal has. This potential, coupled with an extraordinary brain, has enabled us to transcend the limits of our physical structure through the use of tools, machines, and devices. One can be tempted to believe that we are entering a new age, the age of superman or bionic man and woman. If we ignore the fact that our bodies and our feelings haven't changed, we indulge the grandiosity of narcissism. Structured situations also create limits to permissible actions. Presumably, a therapist doesn't seduce a patient. A lawyer doesn't deal behind a client's back against the client's interest. If we deny or ignore limits, we destroy structure. Without structure, a situation becomes chaotic in that anything goes. In the absence of structure, there is no meaning or order.

When structure breaks down in a society, chaos develops, creating an atmosphere of unreality. High inflation, for instance, undermines the value of money, fostering a sense of unreality. Unreality threatens a person's sanity, unless the person cuts off feelings and operates from thinking alone. It is in this way, I believe, that the breakdown of Victorian sexual morality has led to an increase in sex divorced from love or feeling (except sensation). That is narcissism.

Yet an old structure must break down if a new one is to emerge. That is the natural process of growth. We should not, however, delude ourselves into thinking that the breakdown, in itself, represents progress. It holds out the possibility of growth, but there is no guarantee that the new will be better than the old. Historically, the breakdown of a society has sometimes led to a period of darkness before a new light dawns. We may be in for such a time, a new Dark Ages, if we cannot distinguish between order and chaos.

Above all, we should not regard the absence of limits as freedom. A leaf blown by the wind is not free in human terms. A person without emotional ties to people or places is removed, not free. Doing whatever one wants doesn't make one free. Such behavior characterizes insane people, who are swept by the winds of their sensations without an awareness of reality.

The absence of limits results in a loss of the sense of self. Limits are boundaries. We saw in Chapter 7 how the flooding of ego boundaries leads to insanity, where the person no longer knows where the self stops and the world begins. Without a boundary to separate the individual from the environment, there is no self. When a drop of water enters a pond, it is no longer an individual drop. Individuality and selfhood depend on recognized and accepted boundaries and limits. Such boundaries ensure the containment of feelings so that the ego is not flooded, overwhelmed, and lost. Secure boundaries lead to a secure sense of self, one that can base its identity on feelings.

The breakdown of social structure manifest in the disintegration of family life, the lack of respect for authority, and the collapse of established moral principles destroys boundaries, removes limits, and leads to the denial of feeling and the loss of a sense of self. In place of the self, one creates an image to provide some identity. In today's culture, that image is described as a life-style. We are told that we are free to create our own life-styles, in effect creating our own identities. Obviously, there can be as many different life-styles as there are different images. But when one bases one's identity on a life-style, isn't one confusing the artifact with its creator, the house with its occupant, the façade with the feeling self? A house without an occupant is not a home, a life-style without a self is not a person.

The absence of limits today is the product of the tremendous changes that have occurred since World War II, largely as a result of technological developments triggered by that war. A similar change was initiated by World War I. But for most of us, the awareness of this change is a matter of knowing, not feeling. Today's young people cannot appreciate the significance of the changes, because they have no way of comparing the feeling quality of life today with what it was in the early years of this century. Since the way we live not only reflects but also determines who we are, it would seem that the character structure of contemporary youth must be significantly different from that of their forebears. To understand the difference, I suggest we compare early and late twentieth century in terms of the quality of life.

PERSONAL REFLECTIONS ON THE "GOOD" LIFE

As my own life has spanned the two periods, I would like to offer my sense of the difference between them. I grew up in New York City, in an area that has since deteriorated. In my childhood, it was a thriving middle-class neighborhood. My father had a small business in this neighborhood, from which he made a very modest living. As a child, my personal world was limited to the block on which I lived and played. The other kids living on this block were my friends, and the street was our playground. We met whenever we could get out, and there was always something to do or some game to play. There was a streetcar on our block but very few cars or trucks, so we felt safe playing in the streets. Horse-drawn wagons were still the major mode of delivering supplies. I recall a snowstorm that piled up two to three feet of snow and stopped all activity in the neighborhood for days. It took weeks before the men, shoveling by hand, could free the streets of snow. It was a small world but one that seemed stable, secure, exciting, and pleasurable.

My home life lacked some of these qualities. As I have already indicated, the relationship between my mother and father was not a happy one. My mother was ambitious; her motto was "Business before pleasure." My father put pleasure before business, and as a result, his business suffered. He worked hard but never rose above a subsistence level. Like many women with limited funds, my mother also worked hard to make ends meet—shopping, cooking, baking, sewing, etc. There was constant conflict between my parents over money. Sex, however, was at the root of their difficulties, for my mother was as much against sex as my father was for it. As a result, my home life was joyless, although with my father, I had a number of enjoyable times. Neither of my parents had any tendency to violence or to act out, so I was spared that horror. In an earlier chapter, I described how this situation determined my personal development. I became a phallic-narcissistic character, embodying my mother's ambition in my determination to succeed and my father's orientation to pleasure and sex.

Unfortunately, my world fell apart just as I reached puberty. World War I had brought a number of social changes in its wake. The 1920s were boom years, and many middle-class families prospered. Those that did moved to better neighborhoods. Within two years of my thirteenth birthday, the community I grew up in had disappeared. The families of my friends left the neighborhood, but my own family was too poor to leave. One other family was in the same situation, and I became friends with the two boys belonging to it. But I felt like a displaced person; it was a lonely adolescence.

I graduated from college in 1930, just as the Great Depression began. Luckily, I was able to find some temporary work with the census bureau that gave me the hope of building a living. During the Depression years, I worked as an actuarial clerk and then as a schoolteacher. In 1934, I graduated law school summa cum laude and was offered one position as a law clerk at six dollars a week, which I couldn't afford to take. So I continued to teach school for about thirteen years, until I quit to go to medical school.

The decision to go to medical school grew out of my association with Wilhelm Reich and my desire to become a Reichian therapist. I met Reich in 1940 in the course of my search for some understanding of the mind-body problem. On a conscious level, my interest stemmed from my work as an athletic director during summer vacations, but unconsciously it grew out of the need to heal the splits in my own personality. In my ego, I was identified with my mother and her ambitions; on a body level, I was identified with my father and his love of pleasure and sex. I started therapy with Reich in 1942, without fully realizing the nature of my problem. With increasing awareness came the realization that I would have to work on this problem all my life, which I am doing.

The reader may wonder what my personal story has to do with the question of culture and personality. But I belong to two different cultures, and the task of reconciling their opposing values has also been one of my needs. Although my early childhood was post-Victorian, it was still strongly dominated by Victorian morality. I remember when skirts first rose to knee length, and the women who wore them were called finalehoppers. This was right after the end of World War I, and it lasted only a short time. Skirts descended to the floor again, but this, too, didn't last. They rose a second time, giving birth to the flapper. That marked the end of the dominance of Victorian ideals, but I was too young then to appreciate the significance of this change. One change did strike me forcefully because it was close to home. My mother bobbed her hair, as so many women did in the early twenties. Nevertheless, I remember the shock I had when I first saw her with short hair. Many women began to smoke at this time, too, but because my mother wasn't one of them, I put them in a different class.

I grew up with the idea that there were two classes of girls: bad girls, who were sexually free, and good girls, who weren't. I also believed in the double standard of morality that allowed boys to engage freely in sex without opprobrium, but not girls. Although the Great War had struck a serious blow at these distinctions, in my adolescence I was only dimly aware that a new order was emerging. My own world had also collapsed, and I was desperately engaged in rebuilding my identity. I could not foresee that I would become identified with the forces fighting to free sexuality from the restrictions imposed by a patriarchal and authoritarian culture.

But I must confess that just as I was shocked when my mother cut her hair, I was equally shocked when I first saw miniskirts. That is one of the problems associated with change—that although one can adjust one's thinking and behavior to the new reality, the old order persists in one's feelings. If I am to avoid being narcissistic, I must not deny my feelings, which leaves me in a state of conflict with the new morality.

Major changes have occurred in areas other than sexuality. In the 1930s, I was able to buy a car, which no one in my family had ever dreamed of doing. Owning a car gave me a sense of freedom and power, which I desperately needed to support my insecure self-esteem. It also provided some opportunities for pleasure; the roads were not crowded and the countryside was still unspoiled. The automobile represented progress, which for me (as well as for many others) seemed a blessing at the time. Progress also brought a telephone, a radio, a hi-fi system, a TV set, and other devices that promised and gave some pleasure in the beginning. But the pleasure these things initially brought has steadily declined. There are too many cars, and driving has become more stressful than enjoyable. There are too many TV sets, with the result that programs are geared to the greatest number of viewers, which can only be achieved by reducing the quality to the lowest common denominator. The idea that too many or too much kills the pleasure is a major theme of this study. But to limit participation in the "fruits" of progress poses a difficult ethical issue. Who would be entitled to enjoy these fruits and who should make that determination are questions I can't answer. If all God's children had all the material advantages that the rich could afford, the world would not be a fit place to live in. The natural environment would be completely destroyed. It is fast reaching that point now.

To my mind, the quality of life has decreased even as the material standard of living has gone up. More people have more things, enjoy more conveniences, and can go to more places than ever before in human history. Progress promises a healthier life, a better life, one with more excitement and pleasure and in which people can satisfy their wants and indulge their desires without much effort or pain. It sounds like the nearest thing to paradise. It is called the "good" life. It can be represented by snorkling in the Caribbean, drinking rum punch on a sunlit beach, skiing in the Alps, gourmet dining, disco dancing, and free sex. It includes a home in the country, trips to Europe and even around the world, a boat, designer clothes, etc. All one needs is money. And for an ambitious person in the United States, there are plenty of opportunities to make money. This wasn't true in my youth.

In what way has the quality of life deteriorated? Most of us know the answers to this question. We are aware of the pollution of the environment and the exploitation of nature; we sense the pressures of modern life that allow us no time to be: to breathe, to feel, to contemplate; we are constantly reminded of the demoralization of society in the news of crime, violence, and corruption. But I would like to focus on the demoralization of the individual through the loss of the values that were important in earlier times—namely, self-respect and dignity.

These were values I admired when I was a young man, but they were not part of my being. Just as I was split in my identifications between my mother and father, between mind and body, so I was torn by the conflicting desires to be famous (a narcissistic need) and to be a person, a need for selfhood. In a sense, this book is a personal testament to my struggle to realize my selfhood. In that struggle, I have come to appreciate the importance of self-respect and dignity.

One dictionary defines self-respect as "such a regard for one's own character as will restrain one from unworthy action." Another speaks of it as "a proper regard for the dignity of one's character." We are concerned, then, with worth and dignity—which, I believe, are the opposites of money and power.

One example, to me, of a loss of these values is a strike by schoolteachers. I cannot help but feel that being a teacher is a position of honor. That is the way I looked at teachers when I was young. I did not always agree with my teachers, but I respected them. I know that they were also respected in the neighborhood. But in those days, teachers didn't strike or join picket lines, shouting their grievances like abused workers. They were dedicated to the trust they had assumed and took pride in their dedication. In my opinion, that situation changed with the advent of the union and its demand for more money. I was a teacher when the first moves to organize were being made. I was embarrassed that teachers would put their personal interests above those of the children. They lost my respect. But looking back, I can see that respect had become a relatively meaningless word after World War II. It seemed that only power commanded respect, and so teachers organized for power. That would be the major lesson children would learn from their behavior.

In a similar way, strikes by doctors, nurses, and other health professionals seem to me to run counter to the trust they assume for the care of the sick. A doctor is not an entrepreneur, and his or her primary interest should not be a salary. Nursing is a labor of love rather than a labor for hire, and, as such, it may require some sacrifices. But the satisfaction and good feeling one gets from helping another human being in need should more than compensate for the sacrifices.

One can see that I am somewhat old-fashioned in my views, but I also belong to this culture. I can understand the resentment these people may feel at the sight of so many people who have not put in years of training enjoying the "good" life. If the "good" life is there for the grabbing, why not grab it? Perhaps the problem of this half of the century is that there is too much money around. With such prosperity, it seems that the sky is the limit. Without limits, people seem to lose a sense of themselves as responsible individuals—responsible for the welfare of the community and of its members. Each for his or her own is a narcissistic position, not only because it denies the needs of others, but also because it denies the true needs of the self.

DIGNITY AND SELF-RESPECT

One of my patients remarked as he was terminating therapy with me, "I know what self-respect is. I was over-involved with people, responding to their needs and angry when they didn't respond to mine. Now, I am going to take care of my own needs, of my own body. I am going to respect my feelings and honor them."

True respect looks beneath the surface or the appearance to the inner reality, which is the opposite of the narcissistic attitude. By the same token, self-respect is based on an appreciation of one's true or inner self, not on one's appearance or position. We have self-respect when our actions stem from principles or deep convictions rather than motives of expediency or gain. Impressing or manipulating others brings a loss of self-respect, and without self-respect, one doesn't respect others. The narcissistic person has no self-respect.

On a personal level, we lose our self-respect when we learn to manipulate our parents as they manipulated us. We lie and pretend as they lied and pretended. We are seductive as they were. Of course, we have also lost our respect for them. Parents who respect the feelings of a child earn and keep the child's respect. But in our culture, do we really respect anything? Are we not committed to a philosophy that sets success as the ultimate goal and regards any means to achieve that goal as acceptable? If, for example, success means getting a baby to eat, then distracting the baby with a toy while shoving a spoonful of baby food into his or her mouth is perfectly reasonable. In the philosophy of success, the end justifies the means.

Another quality that seems to be lacking these days is dignity. It sounds like an old-fashioned word. I rarely hear it used now. Instead, I hear a lot about power. The pursuit of power excludes the possibility of dignity because power represents the attempt to compensate an inner feeling of humiliation. If I have power, no one dares humiliate me. But like all compensatory mechanisms, the need for power or money confirms and reinforces the inner feeling of humiliation, despite efforts to deny it.

Dignity is a way of carrying oneself. The word stems from the Latin *dignitas*, which means "worthiness." The dictionary lists one meaning as "Character which inspires or commands respect." Character and carriage are related. Carriage and bearing express one's character. People with dignity carry themselves in such a way as to inspire or command respect. It is interesting to note the association of respect and dignity (stemming from their common base in a sense of worthiness). Both are qualities that are missing in narcissists.

There are two aspects to a dignified bearing: the way one moves and the way one holds one's body. It is undignified, for example, to scurry around like a rat looking for a hole. We think of dignified movement as being slow, stately, as if a person had time, time to be and to feel. There is no dignity in the frenetic activity of people in a large city who have no time to spend. There is no dignity in the restless pursuit of pleasure that characterizes the new hedonism. In robbing us of time, today's culture also robs us of dignity. But dignity has no great value in a culture devoted to progress, power, and productivity. Since time is money in modern culture, few of us can afford dignity.

To have a dignified bearing, the body should be straight with the head held high. A stoop-shoulder posture denotes a lack of dignity because it expresses an attitude of being overburdened. The bodily collapse characteristic of a masochistic attitude also denotes a loss of dignity, for it expresses submissiveness.[7] But the erect bearing that expresses a sense of dignity is not a rigid, boardlike straightness seen in some narcissistic individuals. That is a pose. The straightness of a healthy body results from a strong flow of excitation or feeling along the backbone, similar to the process in Kundalini yoga. This charge keeps the head high. The posture also expresses a sense of natural pride in oneself, which differs from narcissism in that it is based on the self, not the image. Such a bearing is possible only if the body is free from chronic muscular tension and, therefore, also free from suppressed conflicts stemming from childhood.

There is an interesting correlation between dignity and sexuality. The same charge that, moving upward, produces the bearing characteristic of dignity provides a sexual charge and excitement when it moves downward in a man. The erect penis is the psychological counterpart of the erect head. But it is not just the charge in the genitals that represents one's sexuality but the charge and the feeling in the pelvis. The pelvis is homologous to the head in the dynamic structure of the body. Just as the head of an animal is held high when it is free and proud, so is the tail. This characterization applies to the woman as well as the man. We describe a person who is vibrantly alive with feeling as being "bright eyed and bushy tailed." In the natural state, the pelvis is carried backward and loose, so that it moves freely with the body's motions. The backward position corresponds to the tail stuck upward. Its opposite is seen in a frightened dog whose tail is tucked between its legs with the pelvis pulled forward.

In the forward position, the pelvis is in a state of discharge. Any excitation flowing into the pelvis will be funneled directly into the genitals. In the backward position, the pelvis will hold or contain the charge. The pelvis can be likened to the hammer of a gun, which is charged by being pulled backward. We say it is cocked. When it moves forward, the gun is fired and the hammer is discharged. Another applicable metaphor is the bow and arrow. It is necessary to pull the bowstring and arrow backward to tense the bow that will provide the force to power the flight of the arrow. With the pelvis held forward, it is very difficult to make the normal sexual movements of thrusting. Such a movement is easy when the pelvis is first pulled back, like the hammer of a gun. When one carries one's pelvis loosely in the back position, one has a cocky (tail in the air) posture. These positions of the pelvis have a bearing on one's dignity. When the pelvis is pulled forward, the natural erectness of the body collapses. You can verify this statement by doing a simple experiment. In a standing position, pull your pelvis forward and note how your body collapses if you don't counter it with an enforced rigidity. Now draw your pelvis backward and observe how your body straightens up naturally. It seems obvious that true dignity is associated with and based on an identification with the body and its sexuality. One of the standard exercises in bioenergetic analysis is the bow or arch position, which helps a person sense the position of his or her pelvis and reduce some of the muscular tensions that restrict its motility. This position will be described below in connection with the process called grounding.

The key to dignity is the sense of having one's feet firmly planted on the ground. Our legs and feet are like the roots of a tree that not only anchor the tree to its reality but also provide the base for the upward thrust of its growth. A person's legs and feet are his support system and provide the foundation for his sense of self. If one has a feeling contact with the ground through one's legs and feet, one is connected to the reality of one's body as an embodiment of his being. Lacking this contact, one is said to be ungrounded—up in the air or in one's head and connected mainly to the images that reside there.

Two exercises are helpful in promoting grounding, as the process of establishing a feeling contact with the floor or ground is called. One is the bow or arch mentioned above. To do this exercise, one stands with the feet about two feet apart, toes slightly turned inward to rotate the thighs, reducing the tension in the buttocks. The knees are bent, the weight of the body is on the balls of the feet, and the body is slightly bent backward. This is easily done if the fists are placed in the small of the back. The pelvis must not be pushed forward but held loosely back. (If the pelvis is held or pushed forward, the line of the arch is broken, interrupting the flow of feeling into the lower part of the body.) One lets the belly out so that breathing is abdominal. If the breathing is deep and easy, one can feel connected to the feet and to the ground. The legs and even the pelvis may vibrate spontaneously if the body is fairly relaxed. The position should be held for at least a minute.

The next exercise is a reversal of the arch and can be done following the arch exercise or independently. The person bends forward until the fingertips touch the ground. The feet are twelve inches apart and turned slightly inward. The knees are bent just enough so that the fingertips touch lightly; the weight of the body is on the balls of the feet. Again, the key is breathing. Without a free and full respiration, very little sensation develops. If the hamstring muscles are tight, as they are in most people, gently stretching them by straightening the knees furthers the sensation in the legs and may induce a spontaneous vibration which may extend to the pelvis. I suggest holding this position for a minute or longer. Sometimes tingling sensations develop in the feet if one hyperventilates, that is, breathes more deeply than one is accustomed to. When that happens, one simply reduces the depth of breathing. Almost everyone reports the vibration experience as a pleasurable feeling. They also report that they feel their legs more than they had previously; they may even sense a better contact with the ground.

I have been doing these exercises regularly for about thirty years. They are not the only ones I do, but they are basic to my exercise program. They have helped me greatly by deepening my breathing, reducing the tension in my body, and giving me a better sense of who I am. My objective is not to improve my figure but to increase the aliveness of my body, which helps me feel better and consequently look better.

THE UNREALITY OF TODAY

Without a sense of contact with the body, as such exercises help provide, one loses one's grounding in reality. And this is what has happened to many people today. The simplest way to characterize the unreality of the modern world is to say that it is bewitched by images. I believe this explains the high regard many people have for fashion models. There seems to be an aura of superiority about a model. The word itself has as one of its meanings "worthy to be imitated" And they are imitated, not only in what they purport to model but in who they are. Twiggy set a style for a whole generation of women. One can argue the question whether the model sets a style or simply displays it. But a model's style is one that many young people try to adopt, that is, to look handsome, exciting, glamorous, outgoing, debonair, passionate, seductive, macho, etc. The important thing is how one looks. And because looks sell, models are high priced if they have that special look. But a model is a person who poses for a living, a living mannequin that advertising people and photographers direct and use. It is not a vocation associated with a sense of dignity, although it need not involve any surrender of self-respect.

But, I wonder, can a person be a model and still be vibrantly alive? I have known and worked with a number of models, men and women. In all cases, I was impressed with the unaliveness of their bodies. Posing was easy for them, for it required little effort to still their expression. Further, their unaliveness didn't distract the reader from the object they were selling. When my wife Leslie and I were living in Geneva in 1949 where I attended medical school, she was recommended by a friend to model clothes in a couturier establishment. The friend was doing the same at the shop and thought that since my wife was very attractive with a fine figure, she would make an excellent model. Leslie wears clothes beautifully, and she had done some modeling in her youth in department stores. At the interview, Leslie modeled several dresses walking in front of the owners. At the end, she was informed that they couldn't use her. They explained that the clothes did very little for her. She would look good in any dress, and besides, they said, the aliveness of her manner would draw attention away from the clothes.

The problem with aliveness is that it can't be translated into an image. By its very nature an image has a static or still quality whereas aliveness can never be static or still. Moving pictures can create an illusion of aliveness but not an image of aliveness, which must be static. Since images can have considerable commercial value, they become very important in a culture in which notoriety and money are dominant values. Because an image is the antithesis of aliveness, the latter suffers when the image becomes all important. Only images can be used to sell goods or services; consequently, aliveness has no commercial value. In a commercial society—a society of images—notoriety and money are closely linked because the popularity of an image is its biggest value.

The connection between loss of aliveness and bewitchment with images is most evident in our involvement with TV and video. We all know that overexposure to television has a depressing effect upon the body's aliveness. Although we are constantly stimulated by images, we have no way of releasing the excitation. The passive viewer must "deaden" his body to stay in control. I have heard a number of people complain that watching television for several hours makes them feel more tired than before. I have experienced this reaction myself. It explains the hypnotic effect the tube has. Once we start watching a program, we continue to watch almost against our will, and we may watch one program after another. Having given ourselves over to the passivity of watching, we soon lose the energy to resume our active life. This process of deadening makes one turn to TV for its stimulation which, of course, creates a vicious circle: loss of aliveness leads to a need for stimulation which in turn produces more deadness.

There are some positive aspects to television. We have all enjoyed some fine programs, a fact that increases our hope that each time we turn on the television something exciting will be presented. But this promise of excitement is, like all seductive promises, only rarely fulfilled. Although fine programming is rare, the seduction of the viewer is effective. Regardless of the quality of the typical program, people are hooked to television.

I believe a major reason for the popularity of TV is that it enables people to escape from themselves. Watching TV has some aspects of a regressive phenomenon. One is passively entertained like a baby, with no response expected and little demand made on the viewer to exercise imagination. If regression, which doesn't lead to a deepening of insight and a forward movement, is one form of escapism, another form is to become so absorbed in the images and story on the screen that one loses contact with the needs and responsibilities of one's life situation. The unreal world of the screen replaces for a time the real world of personal feelings and relationships.

Escapist tendencies are very strong in our society. The widespread use of drugs and alcohol, especially by young people, testifies to this. I believe young people turn on to drugs because they can't handle the overstimulation to which they are subject. Drugs and alcohol offer a way to escape an intolerable situation. Another form of escapism is to become involved in mystical experiences. In such an experience, one feels identified with the cosmos, a universal force, the godhead, etc. The essence of the experience is to transcend or get out of the self, which is believed to restrict or confine the spirit. Mystics attempt to achieve this state of union with the universal force by fasting, the denial of desire, and a detachment from the everyday world, but Western seekers after the mystical experience want to be in both worlds. I do not see their quest as a true spiritual adventure but more as an attempt to escape the self which has become a burden to the person because he or she cannot handle the feelings. In my opinion, this involvement with the mystical is a narcissistic maneuver evident in the fact that many of these individuals regard themselves as superior to the common humanity struggling with the mundane problems of living. Jonathan Livingston Seagull made a similar effort to transcend his mortal existence.

Escapism is also a factor in much of the fascination many people have with space. Movies that portray space adventures and wars have an almost unbelievable box-office appeal, despite the fact that these movies involve strange creatures in unreal situations. People respond to them as if they were more meaningful or real than the actual struggles in which they engage. In space-war fantasies the conflict is always begun by hostile powers as they seek to dominate and subdue a peace-loving democratic people. The fight is always between the good and the bad. The forces on each side, if unreal, can at least be identified. On the other hand, the average person's sense of security and well-being in real life is threatened by impersonal forces that cannot be as easily identified: economic forces like inflation and unemployment, political forces like wars and corruption, social forces like violence and bureaucracy. Against these forces one feels powerless as one did as a child under the domination of parents. One can escape that sense of powerlessness temporarily by becoming lost in outer space where, in the movies, the good and the right win out. What can document the unreality of our times more than this reversal? Images of outer space, which have no objective reality, nevertheless evoke more real feelings than one's daily life on earth.

In his imagination or in reality, the modern individual seems to need a sense of power to overcome an inner desperation stemming from the experience of being powerless as a child and powerless as an adult. But to believe that power can resolve the complex human problems is an illusion. The unreality of the modern world is its faith in power. God has been replaced by Superman. And although Superman is only an image, he represents the belief that with enough power (knowledge and money), a man can set the world right. With enough power, he can control his destiny and determine his own fate. He may need the help of Superwoman to accomplish this task. Her image is rapidly taking shape. This is the philosophy behind the technological revolution that has produced the so-called Age of Information. Given enough information, the sky is the limit to what we can do. The ultimate goal is to eliminate sickness, overcome aging, and conquer death. We will finally become immortal, gods. Is there a greater megalomania than this? Our aspiration for godhood is reflected in our search for omniscience, our striving for omnipotence, and our wish for immortality. But as long as there is a god or some superior force to whom we ascribe these qualities, we stay within the limits of human nature. We recognize that our knowledge is always incomplete, that our power will always be insufficient to affect our fate, that we are mortals. This recognition is the basis of humility and humanity. It permits us to say, "I don't know."

And it allows us to empathize with others, for we admit our commonness. Recognizing and accepting our limits, we become true persons, not narcissists.

The unreality of the "good" life is that despite its appearance and trappings of pleasure, it is joyless. I am not saying that there is no joy in the world. It is missing, however, from this style of life. Looking at the people at the Hyatt Hotel in Kaanapali on the island of Maui, a luxury hotel in a splendid setting, I could see no joy in their faces or bodies. Outside of the children who played in the pool, I saw no spark of exuberant life in the vacationers. I could not sense any real pleasure in their being or doing. Admittedly, this is a general observation, which may not be true for everyone there, but it does support my proposition that the "good" life is more show than feeling.

In my opinion, the unreality of the age is nowhere more apparent than in Las Vegas, which as a location lacks any charm. Yet it must offer something, for people flock to it in great numbers. The big hotels and casinos are done up like Kublai Khan palaces. They are designed to be unreal, fairytale places, where people can get away from themselves. The lights, the music, and the activity bombard the senses, overwhelming one's sense of reality. Obviously, people need this stimulation; it must make them feel alive. And that is the nature of the new hedonism. It is not an obsession with pleasure but a search for stimulation and sensation to overcome the lack of feeling in deadened bodies. The gambling in Las Vegas also serves this purpose. From the point of view of the casino operators, the atmosphere of unreality helps patrons part with their money more easily, for money, too, takes on an unreal quality. Observing the faces of people at the gaming tables or slot machines, I could see the desperation of their desire to win. Theirs is a negative excitement; it doesn't lead to real pleasure.

The concept of negative excitement is germane to the

narcissistic problem. Like everyone else the narcissistic individual needs excitement in his life; but having denied his feelings, he cannot experience the excitement of longing and passion. He seeks his excitement, then, in the challenge of winning or losing, in the struggles for power, and in situations of danger. His excitement is derived from the element of threat—a threatened loss of money, power, or life—and his ability to overcome the threat. However, for the narcissist, winning is less important than not losing. The money he may win in gambling or the power he may gain mean little in themselves. Winning feeds his ego but provides little of the needed pleasure on the body level. The only real pleasure he gets is from the overcoming of danger and the removal of threat. The excitement stems from the negative element in the situation, and his pleasure is more relief than fulfillment.

Pleasure is a life-positive experience.[8] A cool drink of water when one is thirsty is an example of real pleasure. It would be hard to match that pleasure with the finest cocktail. Similarly, any good meal when one is hungry is enjoyable. On the other hand, eating the best meal when one is not hungry can be painful. We have all known the pleasure of being able to give in to sleep when we are tired and drowsy. Yet knowing these simple pleasures, most of us do not organize our lives around them. We eat and sleep by set hours, regardless of our feelings. We rarely let ourselves get really thirsty or famished; water and food are too readily available. In this sense, the material richness of our lives is a handicap to the enjoyment of life. People living closer to a survival level may experience more discomfort, but they will also know the greater pleasure of fulfillment when their basic needs are met.

Desire is the key to pleasure. How much desire one can feel is determined by how alive one is. Dead people have no desire, depressed people have little desire, and older people have less desire than younger ones. Children, being most alive, feel the most desire and have the greatest pleasure when their desires are realized. I have seen my little son literally jump for joy when he got something he wanted very much. He couldn't contain his excitement, it was so strong. That is the secret of joy—to be so excited that one is overwhelmed by it. But to experience joy, one must be free of anxieties about letting go and expressing feeling. Or, to put it differently, one has to be carefree and innocent as a child. Narcissists are neither carefree nor innocent. They have learned to play the power game, to seduce and to manipulate. They are always thinking about how people see and respond to them. And they must stay in control because loss of control evokes their fear of insanity.

I am sure some of us have known moments of joy when our egos took a back seat and the child in us was free to laugh and love. Unfortunately, we lose our innocence too soon, and most unfortunately, we prize this loss. We don't want to be innocents, for that leaves us open to being ridiculed and hurt. We want to be sophisticated—that allows us to feel superior. Sophisticated people seem to have the most fun—partying, drinking, being a little wild, denying limits. What have the innocents got? An open heart, simple pleasures, faith. How much more alluring to have a sharp mind; to know all of life, the lows as well as the highs; to have power, be admired, feel special. The seduction of power is hard to resist, particularly when, as a child, one was hurt and betrayed by those one loved. To sell out the kingdom of heaven for power is a devil's bargain. It is the bargain that the narcissist makes.

NOTES

CHAPTER 1

1. This kind of dissociation is the basic mechanism underlying the schizophrenic process. For a fuller, more detailed discussion of this concept, see Alexander Lowen, *The Betrayal of the Body* (New York: Macmillan, 1967).

2. Theodore I. Rubin, "Goodbye to Death and Celebration of Life," *Event*, Vol. 2, No. 1 (1981), p. 64.

3. Otto Kernberg, *Borderline Conditions and Pathological Narcissism* (New York: Jason Aronson, 1975), p. 264.

4. Ibid., p. 231.

5. Sigmund Freud, "On Narcissism: An Introduction" (1914), in *The Collected Papers of Sigmund Freud*, Vol. 4, ed. Ernest Jones (London: The Hogarth Press, 1953), p. 30.

6. Ibid., p. 45.

7. Michael Balint, *The Basic Fault* (New York: Brunner/Mazel, 1979; orig. pub. 1969), p. 20.

8. Wilhelm Reich, *Character Analysis* (New York: Orgone Institute Press, 1959; orig. pub. 1933), p. 201.

9. Ibid., p. 202.

10. Ibid., p. 189.

11. See Alexander Lowen, *The Language of the Body* (New York: Macmillan, 1971; orig. pub. 1958).

12. James F. Masterson, *The Narcissistic and Borderline Disorders* (New York: Brunner/Mazel, 1981), p. 30.

13. Ibid., p. 12.

14. Ibid., p. 44.

15. Alan Harrington, *Psychopaths* (New York: Simon & Schuster, 1972), p. 18.

16. Ibid., p. 18.

17. See Lowen, *Betrayal of the Body*.

CHAPTER 2

1. Sigmund Freud, "On Narcissism: An Introduction" (1914), in *The Collected Papers of Sigmund Freud*, Vol. 4, ed. Ernest Jones (New York: Basic Books, 1953), p. 32.

2. Christopher Lasch, *The Culture of Narcissism* (New York: W.W. Norton, 1979).

CHAPTER 3

1. Alexander Lowen, *Fear of Life* (New York: Macmillan, 1980).

2. See Alexander and Leslie Lowen, *The Way to Vibrant Health* (New York: Harper & Row, 1977), for a description of the bioenergetic stool.

3. See Lowen, *Fear of Life.*

CHAPTER 4

1. Masterson, *Narcissistic and Borderline Disorders*, p. 72.

2. Ibid., p. 188.

CHAPTER 5

1. For a detailed description of such exercises, see Alexander and Leslie Lowen, *The Way to Vibrant Health.*

2. Sigmund Freud, "The Passing of the Oedipus Complex" (1924), in *The Collected Papers of Sigmund Freud*, Vol 2 (London: Hogarth Press, 1953), p. 276.

CHAPTER 6

1. See Lowen, *Betrayal of the Body.*

2. Alexander Lowen, *Pleasure: A Creative Approach* (Baltimore: Penguin Books, 1975).

3. Jean Liedloff, *The Continuum Concept* (London: Futura, 1975).

4. William F. McKinney, Jr., S. S. Sisoumi, and H. F. Harlow, "Studies in Depression," *Psychology Today*, May 1971, p. 62.

5. See Rene Spitz, "Anaclitic Depression," in *The Psychoanalytic Study of the Child*, Vol. 2 (New York: International Universities Press, 1946); John Bowlby, *Maternal Care and Mental Health* (Geneva: World Health Organization, 1951).

CHAPTER 7

1. David Abrahamsen, "Unmasking Son of Sam's Demons," *New York Times Magazine*, July 1, 1979.

2. Ibid.

CHAPTER 8

1. Sigmund Freud, *Beyond the Pleasure Principle* (New York: Liveright, 1950; orig. pub. 1920), p. 32.

2. Ibid.

3. Ibid., p. 35.

4. Leopold Bellak, *Overload* (New York: Human Sciences Press, 1975).

5. For a discussion of these two modes of existence (one based on feeling, the other on doing), see Lowen, *Fear of Life*.

6. Alice Miller, *Prisoners of Childhood* (New York: Basic Books, 1981), p. 74.

CHAPTER 9

1. Bellak, *Overload*, p. 23.

2. See Lowen, *Betrayal of the Body*, for a more detailed exposition of this concept.

3. Hervey Cleckley, *The Mask of Sanity* (St. Louis: C. V. Mosby, 1955).

4. Ibid., p. 152.

5. Ibid., p. 148.

6. Ibid., p. 153.

7. For a more detailed analysis of the relation between body posture and character, see Lowen, *Language of the Body*.

8. For a more detailed discussion of the nature of pleasure, see Lowen, *Pleasure*.

INDEX